Starfish Leaders

*Stories of
Brokenness and Regeneration*

Rebecca Merrill

First published by Dog Ear Publishing
4010 W. 86th Street, Ste H
Indianapolis, IN 46268
www.dogearpublishing.net

ISBN: 978-160844-593-6

This book is printed on acid-free paper.

Printed in the United States of America

Dedication

I gratefully dedicate this book to my dear friend, Bill Mayo,
who was present, virtually,
at the conception of *Starfish Leaders*
and was my omnipresent North Star throughout the writing
process.
Without his pacing, insight, edits and commentary,
it would not be the book it is today.

Contents

Prologue

Reconciling

January covered New Hampshire with a soft layer of white blanketing the undulating landscape, like a plush wool carpet that had been laid down by an unseen hand. Every inch, as far as the eye could see, lay covered in snow, which continuously swirled, heavy and white over the land and sky, so that I couldn't tell where one ended and the other began. I shifted uneasily in the scratchy velour seat at the front of the Greyhound bus and wearily leaned my face against the cold window. The coolness felt good against my feverish face and for a moment I felt a sense of soothing peace cascade over me. The moment left me as fast as it had arrived, however, and I felt the familiar returning anxiety run the course of my body like a noxious river of poisonous liquid, turning my stomach into a knot, the size and density of a baseball. I couldn't see the road through the window, nor any signs or familiar landmarks, so I startled when the bus driver called out the stop at the Dartmouth-Hitchcock Medical Center in Hanover.

I hurriedly bent down to lace my hiking boots and then stood up, reached into the overhead bin and pulled down my backpack, being careful not to fling a loose buckle into some unsuspecting passenger's face. It was heavy and hard to maneuver, but I managed to hoist it onto one shoulder as I quickly walked to the front of the bus, trying not to delay the driver, because this was a special stop and not a regular part of his route. The driver gave me a compassionate look, but didn't say a word as I stepped down into the foot well and out into the world of white.

I watched the cars that navigated their way slowly through the snow-laden streets, as if they were driving through flat sand dunes. Soon I noticed a clearing of cars and quickly started to cross the road before more traffic rolled towards me, jeopardizing my safe passage. Once across, I shifted the backpack more squarely on my shoulders and started trudging towards the looming hospital building, which I could barely discern through the gray whiteness. After about fifteen minutes of vigorous walking, I arrived at the circular drive in front of the hospital and breathed a grateful sigh, as I took shelter under the covered walkway leading up to the hospital entrance.

I walked through the automatic double doors and headed towards the information desk that filled the middle of a cross-like set of corridors, each leading to a different part of the hospital. Walking up to the counter, I asked a gray-haired volunteer with a kind face where I could find my mother. He looked up her name, identified her room number and then indicated that I should take the curving staircase to my left, between two of the corridors. I thanked him, walked slowly over to the landing and started to climb the stairs, when suddenly I felt intense weariness settle into my tired legs, making it difficult to take each next step.

I pushed through the tiredness and just as I was rounding the last curve of the staircase I looked up and saw my father coming towards me with his familiar sweater-clad body, his monk-like haircut and kind face. Walking briskly, he reached me before I had a chance to move more than two steps in his direction. He offered to take my heavy backpack but I declined, thanking him and letting him know that it would take more energy to take it off than it would to keep it on at that point. I kept walking as he took my hand and walked with me silently towards a door that stood just slightly ajar a little way up on my left. As we walked, I could feel the strength of his warm hand holding mine and quietly thanked God that he and I had such a close bond. It made the other, angst-ridden bond with my mother easier to bear. We stopped just outside of the door and he helped me take off my backpack, indicating that I could go inside by myself for a little while and he would stay outside.

I walked tentatively into the room. There was a hospital bed directly in front of me with a chair on the opposite side and a window above the chair. My mother lay on her side on the bed with her back towards me, displaying an untidy row of ribbon ties running down the middle of her hospital gown. A sheet partially covered her and she lay perfectly still. I quietly walked up to her and put my hand on her arm. It felt dry and hot. I stroked her hair and stood there, uncertain about what to do next. I then heard her faintly whisper my name and I answered, "I'm here, mommy." It felt strange calling her that, but it would have felt stranger still to call her anything else at that point. All vestiges of formality had fallen away when I walked into the room and now I stood there, touching my mother and feeling waves of deep sadness wash over me as I allowed myself to fully acknowledge how close to death she was.

After a long pause, she started to speak. In the next few minutes, the words she spoke began slowly dissolving a decade of encrusted pain and longing, a decade of feeling like an outcast, broken and unloved, a decade of loneliness and heartache. As I stood there for what seemed like an eternity, I had flashbacks of the many times I had tried to reach her by phone, only to have her hand it to my father, telling him that his daughter was on the phone. I remembered the bouquet of roses I sent which went unacknowledged. I recalled the long letter I wrote to her begging for her forgiveness. I remembered countless nights of sheer, unending grief that roiled around inside me, filling me with anguish that erupted in bursts of tears and waves of sobbing. All these memories flashed before my eyes, as I stood unseeing before my mother's dying body.

After this dark musing, I walked around to the other side of the bed so that I could see her face and hear what she had to say more clearly. Her voice had gotten thin and hard to hear, a far cry from the firm, no-nonsense tones of her younger, healthier days. I pulled the chair over to the side of the bed and sat on the edge of it, holding my mother's hand and stroking her hair. I sat and I listened. "Becca," she said, "You and I have had our differences and I know you've felt unloved and misunderstood for a long time." She paused for a breath and the silence hung between us like a sheer curtain separating one side of our relationship from the other. She gathered her energy and continued, "I want you to know that I love you very, very much and I always have. I would have raised the Titanic for you, Becca-love." As she spoke these difficult words, these words that had taken a decade to utter, the tears began spilling over my cheeks and dripping, unnoticed, onto the front of my sweater. I sat there, quietly, letting the words sink in.

The words reverberated inside my head like a shout in an empty cavern, ricocheting inside my mind and creating an echo that lingered. I had prayed and yearned to hear such words for so long. Even a few weeks before, during our family's last Christmas celebration, I had tried unsuccessfully to express my love for my mother and to get her to melt her frozen expression. Sensing that it might be her last such occasion on this earth, I thought I would create a festive ambiance in the large, mostly finished house she and my father had built over the past four years. I reasoned that she wouldn't be able to take any tangible thing with her, but she might remember the sensory experience, so I tied red velvet bows to the chair backs at the dining table and filled the air with the smell of cloves and cinnamon, simmering in a large pot of mulled cider on the stove.

These attempts were not only unappreciated, they succeeded in angering her to the point where she told my father to tell me to stop, just stop everything I was doing to make our house feel like Christmas. I remembered the chagrin I felt as the words sunk in, tears stinging my eyes and a cold pain clutching at my heart. I weakly protested and then, realizing that it would only make matters worse, I silenced myself and mutely started to untie the ribbons. It seemed that I would not, could not, connect with my mother, even at her end. That was then, however, and this was now.

I finally found my voice and said shakily, "It's okay . . . I love you, too, mommy." I couldn't produce another sound after that, so I just sat a little further back on the edge of the chair and held her hand, stroking her fingers gently and crying softly to myself with tears of gratitude for this gift of peace that had come so perilously close to the end of her life that it might not have come at all. We sat like that for what seemed like ages when my father silently entered the room and looked at us with compassion in his eyes. He walked over to my side and put his hand on my shoulder and gently rubbed my back, saying nothing.

We stayed like that, my father, my mother and me, until a nurse entered the room and the scene dissolved into businesslike action on her part, followed by a series of pathos-laden phone calls to relatives and old friends spreading the news. Not long after that, orderlies wheeled my mother out to the ambulance that was waiting to transport her home to die, and hospice was called to come and care for her as the end quickly approached. An intrepid ambulance driver drove for many miles through the wintry landscape, across the state line into Vermont and onto miles of winding secondary roads until he got to the foot of our special hill. He then braved the steep dirt road covered in snow and ice that meandered its way through a mile of maple forest and cow pasture and stopped at the crest of the hill where my parents' recently built house stood, looking out over a broad, snow-encased vista.

The medics strapped her securely on the rolling gurney and pulled it out of the ambulance and onto the frozen ground. They then rolled her up the ramp that turned two right angles until it met the front door. They pushed her inside and through the house, through the restored double antique French doors, past the baby grand piano we had owned since I was little, through the long, window-laced connector and into the back bedroom where her bed stood, the covers turned down. They picked her up carefully, making sure not to get the tubes that connected her to life-giving fluids and pain-killers entangled, and lay her on the bed on her back. She gave a weak smile as she settled into the bed and a look of peace came over her face.

For the next ten days, I spent time with my mother, climbing into bed with her in the morning, holding her hand, singing to her and stroking her hair. At first, she could speak a little, then not at all. Then her eyes communicated with me and then they too stopped functioning. In the end, her hearing was all that was left so I kept a soft, steady stream of talk and song alive, like a lullaby for a sick baby.

I told her things even when I knew she couldn't hear me. I thanked her for bringing me life and for teaching me so many things. I told her stories that I hadn't been able to tell her over the past ten years and I filled in all the gaps and spaces that had emerged like cracks in an ice floe between us, slowly drifting farther and farther apart until the ice split in two and floated away from itself. During those long, quiet, snow-filled days, I reconnected with my mother and freed myself from a life of unending regret. I prayed my thanks and gratitude over and over again to God, who had brought healing to us at the end of her life. I prayed for acceptance and peace. I prayed for her to have a pain-free ending. I held her hands and I lay next to her, day after day, crawling in her bed in the early morning and leaving the bed briefly, only to eat and relieve myself, during the long days of keeping her company.

On January 12, 1996, somewhere around 2:45 in the afternoon, my mother died. She was fifty-nine years old. I had gone to get something to eat and just as I started back across the connector room, my brother emerged from the other side by her room and said simply, "She's gone." The tears started to flow again, but not with the same depth of sorrow or fear or regret as they had before. This time they flowed and flowed, cleansing my soul and resting my heart, as I relaxed and said good-bye to my mother's spirit. The end had come and I had been there almost the entire time. I had not left her side as she lay dying and I had let her know how much she meant to me. And as I lay there, while her body slowly released its hold on life, I resolved to write someday about the power of forgiveness and "the peace of God that passes all understanding." I resolved to tell this story so that others might find strength in their own journeys towards forgiveness and wholeness. I resolved to tell this story so that the pain of a decade could be transmuted into a life-giving message of hope, reconciliation and regeneration. This is my starfish story.

Part One

Shattered Stars

Character cannot be developed in ease and quiet.
Only through experiences of trial and suffering can the soul
be strengthened, ambition inspired, and success achieved.

Helen Keller (1880–1968)

Introduction

Brokenness and Regeneration

An entry taken from Wikipedia tells us, "Sea stars (also known as starfish) are able to regenerate lost arms. A new sea star may be regenerated from a single arm or ray, attached to a portion of the central disk." It is amazing to me that a starfish can actually regenerate entire arms that have been lost or wounded in underwater battles, just from a single remaining arm and a portion of their central disk. The fact that these simple creatures can do such a seemingly impossible feat is a testament to the power of nature to sustain itself. Even more amazing than that marvelous act of regeneration by a starfish is the fact that a creature as complex as a human being can also regenerate the broken, damaged parts that have been knocked about and assaulted by life. If anything in life can be considered miraculous, surely it is the resiliency that nature has built into biological organisms. Throughout this book, I will borrow from this profound and ever-present renewing act of nature and build upon it, particularly as it relates to the transformative process of regenerating leaders.

Starfish Leaders is composed of short stories about five leaders, all of whom are stars in their own life dramas. They have achieved great things and known great success, but they have also experienced great misfortune, pain, suffering and tragedy. The stories unfold at a critical point in the middle of each of their lives, when each of them receives a wake-up clarion call, experiences a moment of blinding clarity and becomes aware that things are not as they should be. Immediately following each of these moments, things start falling apart in significant ways for each character, who then ventures through a valley of deep wounding and pain-based learning. Ultimately, this journey results in a regenerated state of wholeness, an enlarged capacity for greater personal leadership for the world and a reigniting of the shimmering starlight inside of them. However, this newfound leadership capacity manifests itself in entirely different ways than it had before; it becomes merciful, compassionate and outward-focused leadership. These starfish stories are about leaders being led, sometimes kicking and screaming, into the process of their own regeneration.

Many, if not most, of us doggedly resist the painful truth that only by living *through* the process of being broken, and experiencing all that comes with that brokenness, can we achieve meaningful personal growth. Indeed, life-changing transformation often comes from painful experience. When we live through the pain, we often find wisdom, humility, insight and awareness on the other side.

The irony is that while we may need such transformational events to shape a brighter future, we resist paying the price. But, if we will allow it, pain can serve as grist for discovery of beautiful new facets of our selves – created through the alchemical process of turning pain into power, despair into passion and brokenness into a higher purpose.

Because we hate experiencing pain, we often lack the willingness to submit to the regenerative process available for each of us. We humans avoid as long as possible the slow, arduous process of making meaning out of suffering that creates the unquenchable spirit of great leadership. Lee Bolman and Terrence Deal, two authors who are no strangers to suffering, write in their book, *Leading with Soul: An Uncommon Journey of Spirit,* "Leaders cannot give what they do not have or lead to places they've never been. . . The essence of leadership is not giving things or even providing vision. It is offering oneself and one's spirit."[1] So, there's the rub. Without the process of going to painful places we've never been, places most of us would not willingly choose to go, the alchemy of turning our human suffering into greatness cannot happen.

Just to complicate matters, unlike starfish, we cannot create this alchemy alone in our minds, hearts and bodies. In order to grow, we need to find mentors, guides and teachers who will help us along the path of this journey, and that poses yet another obstacle, described here in *Leading with Soul*: "The challenge is finding someone who cares enough about us and our development to be willing to offer an optimal blend of love and challenge" (p. 197). To sum it up: we have to push into the pain and through the personal development process, with the right people challenging and loving us, in just the right blend of toughness and kindness, if we are to regenerate our own metaphorical broken arms. That's a tall order, but certainly not impossible.

To stay with the analogy, let's say for the sake of argument that we humans have five main parts to our lives, like the rays of a sea star, radiating from a "central disk" which we can call our core personality. These rays branch out from the core of our lives, in the form of intellectual, material, emotional, physical and spiritual aspects of life. Let's take a look at these five aspects. At least in the economically developed parts of the world, many of us work extremely hard at keeping the material-financial arm whole, often spending the better part of our lives working to earn money to buy the material luxuries of life; the fast car, big house or club membership that signal our arrival at the threshold of "the good life."

Some of us work diligently on our intellectual-professional ray, in service of advancing and improving the state of human beings in the world. Others of us may pay significant attention to our physical-sensual ray, knowing that fit, healthy individuals are more likely to experience a better quality of life;

[1] Lee G. Bolman and Terrence E. Deal, *Leading with Soul: An Uncommon Journey of Spirit*, New and Revised Edition (New York: John Wiley & Sons, 2001), p. 106.

but more often than not, our bodies become dumping grounds for unhealthy food, drink and stress. Finally, when it comes to our emotional-relational and spiritual-metaphysical rays, we may abandon those broken or badly wounded parts of ourselves, forgetting that our relationships and our spiritual life are worthy of as much, if not more, of our time as the other three aspects.

When we get right down to bedrock truth, we all consciously or unconsciously spend our time according to our priorities. The way we spend our time is a reliable mirror of what we value. For instance, if you were to represent a week in your life as a pie chart, with each slice sized according to the frequency of your primary activities, you might get a virtual stomach ache from the huge slice of the pie representing your fifty-hour work week (your professional-intellectual ray and material-financial ray). You might be a little hungry as you notice the tiny sliver of pie representing the four hours at the gym you get, if you're lucky (the physical-sensual ray). You might get another little slice for your three-hour date night with your spouse and perhaps another three-hour slice of quality time to spend with your kids (the emotional-relational ray). Rarely, you might take a one-hour slice of time with yourself, thinking about what makes life worth living, and perhaps less than a thirty minute slice in conversation with God (the spiritual-metaphysical ray). Actually, if you're like many of us, God probably gets only a few moments of muttered gratitude or anger, as you dash through your day, striving to achieve at work, stay ahead of the taxes you owe, or get supper on the table.

Starfish leaders are no strangers to this kind of schedule. In fact, unbalanced work-life schedules are often assumed to be one rung that must be climbed on the corporate ladder. Paradoxically, this requirement for corporate advancement creates serious collateral damage. Lives lived consistently out of balance exact tolls in the form of broken homes, chronic loneliness, addictions, heart attacks, spiritual despair and an ever-present longing for something better. Logically, just as it's necessary to have lemons if we want to make lemonade, all of these painful situations are the necessary grist for the mill of personal growth. Maya Angelou obviously thought so, when she wrote, "You may encounter many defeats, but you must not be defeated. In fact, it may be necessary to encounter the defeats, so you can know who you are, what you can rise from, how you can still come out of it."

Not a single one of us will get through life undamaged. The shimmering, shattered stars in life are those who have achieved true greatness by learning to use the accumulated damage in their lives to their advantage, building upon the costly lessons learned by surviving times of great struggle and pain and emerging wiser and more authentic. A quote from Ernest Hemingway sums this up well: "The world breaks everyone, and afterward, some are strong at the broken places." In human bodies, when we tear our muscles through consistent, rigorous exercise, we know they can be regenerated into bigger, stronger muscles. Broken bones also often heal stronger at the break point than they were originally. Star leaders emerge through the process of healing in a way that allows them to lead with integrity, wisdom, and resilience. Bolman and Deal express it beautifully: "Tragedy enters every life. Spirit springs from what you make of it. Wounds provide an eye to find new possibilities" (*Leading with Soul*, p. 59).

Through pain and healing we can deepen our compassion, empathy and willingness to serve and to help others. We can also put ourselves back together again, after we've been broken by life, into a new pattern that shines with a more complex and beautiful artistry. Like glass that has been broken into a thousand pieces and transformed into a beautiful stained glass window, we, too, can be magnificently changed by life, with new facets that reflect love and light in more luminescent ways. If we will allow the process to happen, we can be regenerated into far more complex, beautiful human beings through the process of being broken and made whole again.

If we do it right, our lives benefit from our experience and our learning, especially the painful kind, and we become more integrated as we use the self-awareness gained through pain to refine our vision and our humanity. Not one great leader in the entire course of human history has achieved greatness without being broken and regenerating him or her self in new and fresh ways. This is the power of awakening, being reborn, rising like the phoenix from the ashes, rediscovering the possibilities inherent in life by choosing life over death and healing over brokenness. This is the power inherent in Starfish Leaders.

The following stories tell of so-called "successful" individuals who faltered, stumbled and splintered into pieces and then regenerated themselves through the process of spiritual, relational, material, intellectual and physical healing, within the supportive context of the relationships in their communities. The stories illustrate how lives intermingle in ways that we can't always predict, allowing growth to emerge from the most unpredictable of situations, with the help of the most unpredictable of people, illustrating that our deepest healing occurs within our relationships with others. Bolman and Deal assert, "Leadership is a relationship rooted in community. Leaders embody their group's most precious values and beliefs. Their ability to lead emerges from the strength and sustenance of those around them. It persists and deepens as they learn to use life's wounds to discover their own spiritual centers. As they conquer the demons within, they achieve the inner peace and bedrock confidence that enable them to inspirit and inspire others" (*Leading with Soul*, pp. 62–63).

During the course of life we all have wake-up moments. Sometimes they are mild and give us a little jolt. At other times they stop us in our tracks. Each of the following individuals lived, led and was stopped by life in a different way. Each chose to awaken to their potential for living and leading others differently, through the process of developing their self-awareness by seeking healing for their minds, bodies, hearts and souls. Each story tells of leadership talents that emerge looking nothing like the ones that existed before the wake-up moment. The life of James McCloud is one such story.

Chapter One

Spiritual Regeneration

The Story of Ten

James McCloud, M.D., Ph.D., had served as the CEO of a large pharmaceutical company called PharmaCom, Inc., with two thousand employees and offices in the US and the UK for the past four years, but now the honeymoon seemed to be over. With annual revenue of $200M, and a huge growth spurt predicted, Dr. McCloud had his hands full keeping the myriad balls of his life in the air, but he managed to do this with strength and precision, showing no signs of weakness to the outside world. McCloud had always enjoyed the powerful rush of a command-and-control style of leadership and, to be fair, he came by these character traits honestly. The son of Scotch-Irish immigrants who worked hard, drank hard and fought hard, he saw no reason to change those rough habits now.

Dr. McCloud's 6'3" stature and intellectual prowess exuded authority and commanded respect from most people, even when he was young. This had worked in his favor while in college. His teammates voted him captain of the basketball team for four years running. Later, in graduate school he earned his double-doctorate with deceptive ease. He had such great stamina and fierce self-discipline that no one could tell when he was straining to perform; and he never let on, either. His fierce pride perched proudly on the back of his ability to handle whatever was thrown his way. Dr. James McCloud believed in himself, that much was clear. What else he believed in was anybody's guess and many people found him to be just a tad on the cynical side.

Lean and athletic as a college and graduate student and on into his thirties and forties, he now showcased fifteen pounds of extra weight which had accumulated slowly over the past ten years and landed squarely in his mid-section, much to his dismay. He had been just a little too proud of his strong, statuesque figure and this nod towards aging galled him. Fortunately, he still had a full head of thick, curly (albeit gray) hair, cut short and close to his head and he was clean-shaven, even on Saturdays. He looked good in a suit, dressed impeccably and knew it. He was even greeted by name at the boutique men's clothing stores where he shopped exclusively for his custom-tailored suits, shirts and shoes. Dr. McCloud was not the kind of man to leave anything to chance, let alone his image. He shopped, as he did everything, in a very discriminating manner and drove a sleek silver 500 series Mercedes-Benz. A formidable opponent and a shrewd businessman, James McCloud was a sleeping dog most people chose not to antagonize.

Dr. McCloud had just celebrated thirteen years of what he sometimes referred to mockingly as "marital bliss," with his second wife, Susan. In point of fact, he had sworn that he'd never marry again, after the turbulent five-year marriage with his first wife Gen ended in a vicious and costly divorce. However, his commitment to this personal oath was short-lived when his "animal instincts" got the better of him and he found out fourteen years ago that he and Susan were pregnant with Mariel. At that juncture, he had concluded that he might as well bite the bullet and get married again, if only for his baby girl's sake.

James McCloud had one son by his first marriage with Gen, named Paul, age seventeen, who was the spitting image of him, though he had a much more introverted and sensitive personality. He had accrued two teenage stepsons from his wife Susan's first marriage: Nathaniel, also seventeen, and Pete, fifteen. At the advanced age of fifty-seven, he often grumbled loudly that he was too old for the kinds of arguments that were inevitable in a house full of kids. In secret, however, he admired Paul, who was a chip off the old block in almost every way—looks, smarts and athleticism—and he openly adored Mariel, his precious angel whom he begrudged nothing. He reluctantly tolerated Nathaniel and Pete, but nobody would have said they were close.

While outwardly modest, Dr. McCloud sometimes congratulated himself on being that rarest of rare breeds, a classic renaissance man, equipped with a prodigiously keen intellect, an ability to listen deeply for subtext, meaning and intent, an endless curiosity that kept him forever asking probing questions and a great knack for getting to the heart of things. He had an eye for detail and an ear for logic that allowed him to point out inherent inconsistencies in the strategies that his vision team prepared for him. He also boasted an inexhaustible store of energy and an ability to plow through work that would tax two or three other men. While at University, he came by his nickname, "Ten," honestly, consistently earning perfect test scores and graduating *summa cum laude,* with high honors and a double major in Bio-Chemistry and English Lit. The nickname was so apropos, he had not been able to shed it, despite his advancing age and accumulating achievements.

Despite his dominant and sometimes acerbic personality, Ten had no enemies, or at least none of which he was aware. Then again, he didn't have anyone whom he could honestly call a best friend, either. Sadly, his relationship with Susan, who had once been his confidante, had deteriorated over the past year because of the business pressures inherent in rapid corporate growth and Ten's concurrent need to spend inordinate amounts of time on his work. While he was not one to dwell on the prospect of failure, nevertheless he often privately wondered whether his second marriage would survive the grueling leadership demands that lay ahead.

The greatest threat to his marriage lay with Ten's difficulty in finding time for the things that he professed mattered most to him. Susan most often got short shrift when time was scarce and she had even become somewhat dejectedly accustomed to spending her evenings alone, after Mariel was in bed and the older kids were in their rooms doing homework. Ten felt badly that he missed the chance to have intimate conversations with her on most evenings, but he felt even worse about not spending time with Mariel, whom he had inadvertently neglected recently, because she had almost always been put to bed by the time he got home from work.

Ten's health was good for a man of his age but he had recently fallen off of his routine four mornings a week at the gym, needing to use the time between 6:00 and 8:00 for catching up on the backlog of emails and other paperwork that never seemed to diminish, regardless of how much effort he put into it. He also had no time to read and reflect, keep up with industry trends or develop friendships with other CEO-Scientists in the field of Big Pharma. And it almost went without saying that his spiritual life was non-existent.

As a child, Ten had been raised in the Presbyterian Church and had attended with his mother until he was old enough to refuse to attend and big enough that she couldn't force him to. Ten just couldn't square being a scientist with being a Christian and he didn't want to waste his time reading anything that might convince him otherwise. He didn't see the need for what he considered mindless religious dogma, or putting faith in anything other than the scientific method. He supported his stance with the mostly valid argument that many, if not most, of the world's wars and long-standing hatred between nations had been caused by religious zealots, not scientists. On this subject, as on many others, he logically concluded that he stood on firm ground and saw no reason to debate the issue.

Lately, Ten felt as if he had landed in the midst of what he could only call a late mid-life crisis; he had slowly started to recognize that his old ways of handling the responsibilities and obligations in his life weren't working anymore. For starters, he knew that he needed to reprioritize how he approached the avalanche of work that greeted him every morning, long before his day had officially begun. Making matters worse, the chairman of PharmaCom's board had begun to question Ten's ability to meet the demands of the CEO role and Ten knew that unless he promptly proposed a strategy to redirect the company's global marketing, in light of intensifying competition, he would be facing early retirement. Given the state of the economy, this prospect was an aggravating challenge that he didn't relish, especially with everything else going on.

Ten's budding crisis manifested itself as complete exhaustion, on all fronts. Mental exhaustion appeared as an uncharacteristic indecisiveness and a strange desire to side-step difficult conversations with members of his executive staff. Borderline high blood pressure, coupled with diminishing energy at the end of each workday, indicated increasing physical exhaustion. Emotional exhaustion became evident in his increasing irritability and short fuse with everyone, save Mariel. Lastly, spiritual exhaustion, fueled by an existential crisis of sorts, manifested itself in such a way that everything seemed to have lost its intrinsic meaning and value. It had gotten to the point where Ten had even found himself uncharacteristically contemplating taking a year-long sabbatical to figure it all out.

Ten had become increasingly impatient with his wife Susan's persistent anxiety and feelings of neglect. Consequently he found himself disappearing into his office on weekends and immediately after dinner, on the rare nights that he actually ate dinner with the family. Sadly, he didn't bother to ask her what thoughts and feelings underlay her anxiety because, to be brutally honest, he didn't really care. His own feelings had become blunted and he didn't see the need to go digging around inside Susan's head to find out what she was feeling any more than he wanted to dig around inside his own. His relationship with his son, Paul, and his two stepsons, Nathaniel and Pete, had become distant and guarded, and Mariel had shied away from him when he came home, preferring to stay out of his way. Ostensibly, she was doing her homework and didn't want to be interrupted, but he knew that she was hurt by his chronic absence.

Waking Up

"Ouch!" Ten said as he nicked himself shaving. Pausing to dab the blood with a tissue, he gazed at the weary face staring back at him from the bathroom mirror and realized that he hadn't noticed how old he had started to look. His eyes were tired and had more visible crow's feet crinkling around their edges than he had seen before. "Things have just got to change," he muttered to himself as he dug around in the drawer for a band-aid to protect the cut. Just as he found one and was sticking it on his now bloody chin, his cell phone rang. Ten reached over to answer it, cursing under his breath and threatening that it better be something really important, or he was going to be giving somebody a piece of his mind they weren't going to appreciate.

Ten barked hello into the phone and then winced when he heard his ex-wife's voice. He hadn't heard from Gen in six months, since they had their last fight over Paul's deteriorating performance in school, and the fact that she was calling today could only mean bad news. At this moment, she was sobbing and speaking in brief bursts of words that didn't make any sense to him. All he could make out was his son's name, Paul, the word hospital, and then more wailing. "Christ," he murmured under his breath, "I hope Paul hasn't gone and done anything stupid, like taking out my Mercedes and running it into a telephone pole." Ten knew that Paul had been sulking and angry whenever he was over at their house, and in the back of his mind he was bracing for some retaliatory behavior from Paul who had been grounded from using the family car after being caught with a bag of pot in his locker. "Goddamn kid isn't even smart enough to hide the stuff where he won't get caught. I wasn't that stupid when I was half his age."

"Well stop crying, would you!" he growled. "What on earth has happened? It can't possibly be that bad." Gen took a gulp of air and started to speak between sobs. "Paul overdosed on drugs. I found him in his room with the music blaring. He was unresponsive when I tried to get him to talk to me. I panicked and called 911 and they started to pump his stomach on the way to the hospital, but it was too late to get much of it out of his system." She paused, trying to steady her quavering voice, and Ten felt a cold chill run down his spine. "Where is he now?" Ten asked in a dead-calm voice. "In the ICU. It's very serious. I really need you, Ten. Please, don't let me down now." Ten paused in thought, calculated how much time it would take for him to get over to the hospital, check on Paul, comfort Gen with a quick hug, and then head back to his office where he was prepping for the board meeting this afternoon.

"Okay! Okay," he said, as his voice changed and softened and he tried to soothe Gen. He still loved her, although he hadn't thought about that buried feeling in years, and he still hated it when she cried. "Let me just finish shaving and I'll get over there as fast as I can." Ten hung up and grimaced at his harried image in the mirror, half-shaven and half-dressed, standing in the middle of the bathroom. He certainly didn't look or feel like the bulletproof CEO image he had sold so successfully to the world. "I can see this going downhill fast," he thought as he finished shaving and quickly dressed, grabbed a cup of coffee and walked briskly out the door and into the garage where he started up his Mercedes and pulled quickly out into the street and off to the hospital.

When Ten arrived at the ICU he found Gen, her arms wrapped protectively around herself, standing just outside the door to Paul's hospital room. He walked up to her and touched her lightly on the shoulder. She turned towards him and he noticed the lines of worry etched on her once smooth and lovely face. "How is he?" Ten asked, quietly. She smiled a wan smile as she turned towards him and said in a quiet voice, "They think he'll live, but they're not sure if he'll ever be able to regain his cognitive functioning. Right now, he's not in a coma but he is very unresponsive." She tried to keep up the false bravado but then collapsed into Ten's arms, sobbing softly and moaning to herself.

Ten checked his watch and noticed that he only had a few hours before his early afternoon board meeting. He looked at Gen and then through the half-opened door where Paul lay in the hospital bed with a breathing tube in his mouth, his eyes closed, his long, lean body looking frail and all the color drained from his usually tanned and ruddy face. At that moment Ten made a decision that would forever change the trajectory of his life: he decided to call the board chair and cancel the board meeting. He actually wanted to stay at the hospital with Gen, to provide comfort for her and be there to monitor Paul's progress and make sure the doctors were doing their jobs appropriately. To say that this was a monumental shift in Ten's value system and typical behavior would be an understatement. Ten never let life ride him off the rails, but even he couldn't soldier on with this drama unfolding. As much as he didn't like to admit it, he was starting to feel the tiredness and sadness seep into his body, deadening his nerves like the poisonous substance that Paul had so recently ingested. Besides, he knew that he wouldn't be able to maintain his composure and it would be pointless to pretend otherwise. Ten wasn't a man to give up or give in, but he felt as close to those feelings now as he ever had in his life.

Breaking

When Ten woke up, he realized that he'd been sleeping fitfully on one of the hard benches in the hospital chapel on the main floor, two floors below where Paul lay motionless in his toxic state of catatonia. How long Ten had been lying there, he couldn't be sure because he hadn't checked his watch when he walked in and had no idea what time he had fallen asleep. He peered out the double doors into the hospital hallway and all was quiet. He saw a hallway clock and noticed that it was a little past one in the morning, "deep in the bowels of the night," thought Ten poetically. He felt strangely light-headed, as if he was having an out of body experience. "It must be the lack of sleep and food," he thought absentmindedly, as he promised himself a solid breakfast in the hospital cafeteria when they opened at six.

As he sat, bowed down with tiredness, and gazed at the stained glass window in front of him, softly lit from behind with incandescent light, a great sense of peace came over him. He had no idea why, but there was a deep feeling inside of him that everything would be okay, no matter what happened. Ten recognized this as a spiritual moment and laughed as he shrugged his shoulders and acknowledged it for what it was. "Perhaps I'm getting soft in my old age?" he thought. Who knows, perhaps he recognized in this moment that he needed to believe in something other than science. He knew for sure that science and medicine had done everything they could for Paul. "The rest of it," as others had reminded him, "is in God's hands now."

Just as Ten was collecting his thoughts and gathering his wits about him, a nurse knocked on the door and quietly walked into the room with a look on her face that didn't bode well. "What's the matter?" asked Ten as he stood up to greet her. "It's your son, Paul." She took a deep breath and with a voice of deep sadness said softly, "He's passed on." She paused. "I'm so very sorry, Dr. McCloud. Please let me know if there's anything I can do to help." She stood there in the stillness, waiting, as she watched all kinds of emotions play across Ten's face, the last of which was a look of excruciating anguish.

Ten gave a strangled cry and collapsed back onto the bench with his face in his hands, his shoulders heaving in unison with the sounds of his crying. He cried hard for fifteen minutes as the nurse stood patiently near him with her hand on his arm, prepared to offer whatever solace she could with the few means at her disposal, namely her presence and her physical touch. After some more time had passed, he turned to her with a look that softened the craggy lines of his handsome face and said, "It's okay. It'll be all right. You can go now. Really. I'll be fine." The nurse looked at him with concern and then gave one last squeeze to his arm and glided back out through the doors of the chapel on silent feet. She had witnessed this scene more times than she cared to remember and it always hit her hard, no matter how many times she experienced the grief of a parent crying for a lost child. "One of the saddest losses a human being can ever experience," she thought to herself sorrowfully as she walked slowly down the hall.

Regenerating

Almost a year later, Ten looked up from what he was doing and realized that he hadn't cried in at least a week. The work that he had been doing for the drug rehab center over the last nine months had taken every ounce of his attention and passion and he hadn't been keeping track of his emotional, spiritual, and physical breakdowns the way he had right after Paul had died. "Thank God for that," he thought grimly as he remembered the unbearable pain that seared his body for months after the funeral, each time Paul's memory crossed his mind. "I wouldn't wish that pain on anybody. Enough to drive a person to drink," he thought. Then he laughed a wry, self-deprecating laugh as he realized the existential absurdity of his last thought. "Old habits die hard," he said to himself compassionately as he reached for his coat and prepared to leave the clinic.

After Paul's death, Ten had gone through every negative feeling that was humanly possible: guilt, rage, anguish, fear and despair. Of course, the grief counselor, Amy, whom he had finally agreed to visit, had told him that there are no "negative" feelings, just more or less painful ones. He couldn't ever agree with that neutral assessment of his feelings, for they scoured and scarred him like a high-powered chemical cleanser until he felt like vomiting or collapsing, both of which he did upon occasion. Slowly, patiently and persistently, however, Amy was able to probe into the darkness of his grief and help him light a small candle of hope.

How she did this he would never know, but he felt as if it must have been an act of God because never in the time that he had been grieving did he think he would ever feel hope or optimism again. Forgetting his business, his friends, his family, even Mariel, Ten had fallen into a deep, dark night of the soul; a depression so profound that at times Ten couldn't even speak, but only moan, like a wounded animal. In that dark space, Ten knew instinctively that the only way out of that unspeakable place of pain would be through God, whoever or whatever God was. Anything else would test the full capacity of the human mind and heart to heal, and still leave it wanting, insufficient to bridge the gap between his pain and the hope that lay beyond it, always out of reach.

After a seemingly endless period of grieving, Ten started to come back to life. He started to want to wake up in the morning, to eat, to hear about the news of the world. His business days were over; that had been arranged mercifully quickly as the board had stepped in, quickly appraised the situation and appointed an interim CEO who could run PharmaCom until they had time to put together a search committee for a new CEO. Now Ten's only job was to take notice of the new day, to see with new eyes the beauty in the face of his wife Susan and to hold his daughter Mariel close to him as he smelled her soft hair and felt her small frame encircled by his strong arms.

His new leadership challenge was to repeatedly remind himself why living was a good idea. Amy had helped him to see that his life was still valid and valuable by encouraging him to spend time with others who were in even worse shape than he was. "Hard to imagine," he had thought bleakly at the time, but still she had a point and his compassionate actions seemed to be bearing spiritual fruit as he diligently went to the class for new volunteers at the drug rehab center. He had also eased his conscience by giving a large financial gift to the center. With it they had created a new recreation and exercise space, an addition that had been built almost overnight, it seemed to him. "At least my money is good for something positive," he told himself comfortingly.

The strangest part of the process of completely falling apart was that all the things that had meant so much to him meant nothing now. He hardly ever thought about the job he had left at PharmaCom, and when he did it was with deep relief that he wasn't there anymore. He didn't think about what he wore, what he drove or with whom he had lunch. Nothing that used to matter even showed up on his internal radar screen anymore. Instead of always thinking about himself, his power and position in the world, he now thought about other people and their feelings from a place of deep empathy and compassion.

Now, he paid attention to the flight of a yellow goldfinch as it flitted its way across his backyard. He noticed the color of the sky in the evening when he sat on the front porch with Susan, Mariel and the boys and ate a simple supper of fish, good bread and fresh vegetables from his garden. He noticed the sound of the wind in the trees when a storm was brewing and felt the change in air pressure as it dropped, ushering in the sheets of rain that were such a familiar part of the weather patterns where he lived. He noticed himself praying both silently and aloud, as he talked to God about what he was supposed to do next with his life. All certainty had left him and the only thing left for him to hold on to now was the love he felt for his family and his young, faltering, but still present faith that if it were not for God, he would have gone the same way Paul had, into what felt to him like a deep, dark hell; never to be redeemed, never to know real love or real peace.

It had all come at an astoundingly high, gut-wrenchingly painful price, this newfound knowledge of the spiritual side of himself. "But for all that," he thought to himself, "I wouldn't give it up and go back to the life I left behind." He cringed as he thought about the prison he had created for himself, the loneliness of the long nights of working late, the emptiness and hollowness of the praise he got from the board when he had made a successful business maneuver. Now these were all things of the past, and good riddance to them.

Ten shifted in his chair as he came out of his afternoon reverie. It was late afternoon and almost time for the kids to be coming in for dinner. He loved this time of the day more than any other. It was the time when the lights went on inside their home and inside his heart. It was the time when he paid attention to everything that really mattered to him and gave thanks that he had more life left to be grateful for, more time left with his family and more time left to do good by helping other parents and families through the pain of loss due to drug addiction and abuse.

He had a new leadership passion now, and for once it was not about him at all, not in the least. Now he passionately spoke words of healing and wisdom to parents who didn't know what they were heading for, who didn't know that the long road ahead was one they should avoid at all costs. His was the passion of the newly converted and he spent most parts of most days at the rehab center, speaking with parents and telling them his story. If he could save just one child, just one parent, from the horrific pain that he had been through over the last nine months, it would make his entire life worth something. That much he knew. He closed his eyes, said a silent prayer of thanks and went downstairs for dinner, a smile on his lips and a soft whisper of hope in his heart.

Chapter Two

Material Regeneration

The Story of Zen

Henry Donald Lloyd, M.Div., a second-generation Japanese-American whom everyone called Zen, both because of his ethnic background as well as his usually calm and easy-going personality, was the senior pastor of a contemporary suburban Christian church in a growing metropolitan area. To Zen, the term "senior" hardly seemed a fitting descriptor for his youthful, energetic persona, especially because he was so popular with the younger crowd, so he privately referred to himself as the "leading" pastor, even though he could never convince anyone else to adopt that nomenclature. Zen loved being the center of attention and clearly realized that his popularity was a big part of the new church's drawing power, so he capitalized on it whenever and wherever he could. On more than one occasion, he would get a little rush when he overheard glowing reports from members and visitors alike, speaking in admiring terms of his personal appeal, charisma and the compelling and spirited engagement of his sermon delivery.

While proud of his charming persona, he tried to contain any outward appearance of conceit, preferring to have others believe he was humbly deploying his God-given gifts in service to his spiritual calling. Besides, these personal traits were valuable and certainly necessary for the growth that Zen envisioned for his church. Zen acknowledged his internal struggle with pride, but rationalized that he was merely using the gifts and talents hat God had given him to their greatest advantage.

Zen could truly say he had lived a charmed professional life thus far, precisely because he could almost always obtain whatever he wanted or needed for his church by applying his persuasive personality and banking on the goodwill he generated within his church to get his needs met. Who was he to argue with the church's obvious success? God was clearly leveraging his considerable talents in the world of church ministry. In sum, on most days Zen felt blessed by the God he loved and served and knew he was right where he was meant to be.

Zen stood about 5'8" tall and had a stocky, muscular build, which added to the impression of sturdiness that he conveyed through both his personality and his presence. While not an imposing physical specimen, his powerful personality more than compensated for what he lacked in stature. He wore his dark hair cut very short, in an almost military style buzz cut, and sported a small goatee that he promised himself he would shave off when he reached the ripe old age of forty. It seemed a little sophomoric to him that he still liked the goatee, but he had such trouble growing any facial hair that he was proud of the beard he had finally grown and couldn't quite come to grips with shaving it off. Besides, he reasoned, it added to his hip image and as such, was a valuable marketing tool.

Despite almost hitting the forty-year-old milestone, Zen dressed in blue jeans and Christian t-shirts in order to appeal to the twenty-something crowd, his targeted age group. He had a clear understanding of the social media and networking tools that kept them occupied, 24/7, and aggressively employed these tools in his outreach to this select demographic group. Responsive to the current cultural vibe, he also attracted large crowds of younger students and growing families who appreciated his refreshing message and preaching style.

Zen's enthusiasm, incredible ability to motivate and emotionally connect with his congregation and his uninhibited energy and willingness to share his most vulnerable stories forged bonds with his young congregants. Indeed, it was not lost on Zen that he had created a viral buzz in the local community about the new church in town and the larger-than-life minister who had made it all happen. He felt deeply satisfied with himself, save for one growing concern, namely the chaotic church finances; however, he assuaged his growing angst by rationalizing that he was making God "cool" again and that was worth it, whatever the cost.

Zen had been married for eleven years to Cecelia, whom he considered to be his best friend and soul mate. They met during their clinical pastoral education internship and stayed together while both of them completed seminary, marrying just after they both got ordained. Zen and Cecelia enjoyed collaborating together while creating new and different worship services, providing pastoral care and community outreach. However, despite their proximity during the work day, he and Cecelia seemed to have drifted apart lately due largely, he thought defensively to himself, because of his drive to raise money and finish funding the new church building which had just recently been completed. A thing of beauty with its modern architecture and soaring arches, it mimicked the Gothic cathedrals of the past, but with a warmth and comfort of a church half its size. It was meant to honor God, but it had Zen's fingerprints all over it. Zen was indeed proud of the new church building and the community that he had nurtured and grown over the years—perhaps too proud, but in his mind rightfully so. They were the hard won results of his ongoing labor of love.

However, as he would soon learn, these prizes had come with a steep price and one he had not intended. For starters, Zen had sacrificed a lot of his discretionary time over the past two years on the project, time that he would have otherwise spent with friends and family, and he knew his relationships were starting to deteriorate. The nagging feeling that gave him the most heartburn was the growing mountain of debt that the church had incurred during the building process. Zen knew God could move mountains, but this particular mountain remained an imposing obstacle. Zen had never quite been able to keep himself or his general contractor disciplined about unplanned spending. More to the point, the project consistently went over budget on everything from the marble tile in the lobby to the ornate stained glass in the sanctuary, with his full knowledge and often at his stubborn insistence.

Zen would usually calm his niggling fears by reassuring himself that he could continue to build the church community, ask for increased donations and inspire people to go beyond their initial pledges to make up for the growing difference between the capital campaign funds and what was left to be paid on the loan. What he had accomplished thus far seemed likely to be much harder than what remained, or so he ratio-nalized. But in certain moments, when the clarity of the debt gap crashed upon him, he knew he was kidding himself. The debt had surged past the million-dollar mark due to the extremely high interest rate they had accepted and the chronic overspending for enhancements to the original design. Of course, as a start-up church, Zen's financing hadn't qualified for an attractive rate; they simply had an insufficient credit history to reassure the banks of their ability to repay the loan.

Zen figured that God would lead him out of this valley and the mountain of debt would be chipped away somehow. It had to be. Increasingly, however, the seductive veil of denial that shimmered between him and his worries was wearing thin. He was getting precariously close to an inescapable collision with reality. As much as he tried to avoid the topic and go about business as usual, he knew he was on a downhill slide, straight into an icy lake, and the wake-up moment wasn't going to be pretty. Since childhood Zen had been an expert at whistling in the dark whenever fears beset him. "All will be well, and all manner of thing will be well," he would say to himself, quoting the T.S. Eliot lines from *The Four Quartets.* Or at least he hoped it would be, but he was running out of air and time as he nervously anticipated his financial day of reckoning.

Early in their marriage, Zen and Cecelia had agreed to raise four foster children from the local foster and adoption agency. Terry was now eleven, Tina, nine, Jake, eight and Holly, eight, and they had been lucky enough to have one biological daughter, Stephanie, age seven, who came as a complete surprise to them when they weren't paying sufficient attention to the issue of pregnancy or birth control. The children just added to the energy and excitement Zen felt on most days, but every now and then the sheer magnitude of the debt he had incurred on behalf of the church, as well as the multitude of competing responsibilities as a husband, father, pastor and counselor, would tire him to the point of exhaustion, which started to show up in what seemed to be a persistent low-level of irritability, flaring up at the most inopportune times when he got frustrated, especially with the finance committee.

Zen's wife Cecelia was just the opposite of Zen in terms of personality style. Quiet, introspective and completely uninterested in the limelight, she exuded a quiet confidence and sense of inner peace that Zen was initially attracted to when they were courting. But now she was growing increasingly impatient with him, feeling as if he was not really present when he was at home and that he was becoming more and more wrapped up in promoting his image and expanding his reach into the mission field. She worried that she and the children were becoming an afterthought and felt sad that she and Zen didn't have the sweet, intimate sharing that they used to have each night, after the kids had been put to bed. She had told him repeatedly that they needed to get some marriage counseling but Zen had resisted, saying that he was the counselor, not the counselee, and that he knew all about marital dynamics and didn't need anyone telling him how to be married. Zen and Cecelia had come to an impasse, one that had not gone unnoticed by some of the more observant members of the congregation.

Despite his nickname and general proclivity to being a relatively relaxed and casual individual, being truly at peace was Zen's major psychological challenge. Resting and finding time for prayer and reflection in the small interstitial spaces that existed between the competing demands made by his congregation became a luxury. What with answering email, the church blog, his pastoral care duties and the sermon writing that were all vying for his time, even his advanced multi-tasking capabilities were over-taxed. Thus, his exhaustion became the polar opposite of his enthusiasm and Zen swung erratically between those poles, causing a growing sense of alarm and concern among some members of his flock.

Usually, Zen experienced a deep sense of pleasure when he engaged with people and they warmed in the sunlight of his good will and infectious good humor. It felt good to be wanted and needed and he was a classic caretaker, paying more attention to the wellbeing of his flock than he did to his own. However, his penchant for caretaking had now caught him running on empty more than he cared to admit. His difficulty setting and holding himself accountable for personal time boundaries and his tendency to get distracted and excited by every "bright, shiny object" that crossed his path only compounded the problem.

Zen had built his church from the ground up based on dogged determination, infectious energy and enthusiasm and an openness that allowed him to connect with anyone and everyone. However, his ministry team was beginning to worry that people were attending church because of Zen, rather than because of God. They were concerned that the church was starting to become a "quasi-cult" based on Zen's charisma. The ministry team had even had several conversations about how Zen's personality was starting to become a liability.

Zen privately acknowledged that he loved the attention and the rising popularity that was evident by the number of people who read his blog or listened to him on his internet podcasts and argued publicly with the church elders that God had created his personality and God had blessed him with success, so who could argue? After much spirited debate, leaving Zen more than a little deflated, he ultimately agreed that he would try to deflect some of the attention that was focused on him back to what the real focus should have been all along, namely, God's love. He pledged to work earnestly towards an attitude of genuine humility while continuing to preside over the church.

The lingering problem however, was that Zen wasn't exactly sure he wanted to give up the spotlight, nor how to let go of the high that he got by being adored by so many fans. He had started to become somewhat moody as he tried to figure out how to be authentic without being a cult figure. And he tried to create distance from his congregation by toning down his naturally extroverted style of interacting but only succeeded in appearing depressed and listless. He realized that he had become trapped by his own personality and didn't know any way out. Zen accurately had diagnosed the problem as an insatiable desire for attention and knew that his love of the spotlight took over whenever he was preaching. And, thus, what began as a worship service always seemed to morph into The Zen Show.

During worship services he positively surged with the energy and love that he felt coming to him from his congregation, oscillating with his outpouring of love for them. The more they loved him, the easier it was for him to love them. However, at the end of the day on Sundays he experienced an intense letdown from the contact high he got when he preached and he had a very hard time getting to the level where he could hear and respond to the day to day concerns arising from the congregation during the week. He was feeling spent, and only the highlight of Sunday mornings abated that sense of personal depletion.

Zen had achieved much, it was true, his ministry team assured him: he had raised money for and presided over the building of a beautiful new church building; his church was now ranked as one of the fastest growing churches in his region; and he had become a high-profile member of his local community, active on two non-profit boards and present at almost any fund-raising event for charity that might give him a stage to promote the church. But Zen had reached the point where he realized that his mind and heart were fully engaged in what he was doing but his relationships, body and soul had been sorely neglected in the process . . . and more damagingly, so had the church finances.

Waking Up

Zen rushed out of his office with his latest sermon in his hand, ready to head off to an important lunch meeting. He was sweating hard and realized that he was breathing hard as well. "Damn," he muttered under his breath as he noted he had strayed farther and farther from his New Year's intention to treat his body as God's temple. "If this was God's temple, then God was certainly living in a lower-middle-class neighborhood," he thought somewhat self-deprecatingly. He made a mental note to ask one of the members of his congregation who was a physical trainer and triathlete to help him out with a training program and vowed to faithfully follow it this time. That would also be a great way to get rid of some of the stress that he had been car-rying around in his back and shoulders, he thought. He had already been to the chiropractor three times this month and still had experienced no relief from the nagging low back and neck pain that had dogged him for weeks. He knew that his body was too young to feel this damn old.

Actually, if he were scrupulously honest with himself, he knew exactly when and why the pain had first started. It was the day that he had met with the bank to discuss refinancing the church's building loan at a lower interest rate. "Those bastards wouldn't even give me a chance to explain my situation," he thought bitterly and in a most un-Christian-like manner. "They just looked at the numbers on the church's Profit and Loss state-ment and rejected my request out of hand. That's why bankers and lawyers actually deserve the reputations they have," he grumbled cynically.

Of course he wasn't any too happy with his own behavior of late. He had narrowly dodged a bullet when certain outspoken members of the building finance committee had asked him to share his plan about how to handle the church's budget deficit and soaring operating costs, but he knew he couldn't avoid the conversation forever. "I know. I'll try a couple more banks before I give up and face the firing squad empty-handed," he thought hopefully. Perhaps the new community bank that had just been started across town by a member of his own congregation would help him out. He started to feel a bit of smug satisfaction in that moment, knowing he could rely on his trusty and time-tested personal powers of persuasion to save the day. He hadn't run out of options yet. Or so he thought.

"Damn, damn, damn," he said aloud as he snapped his seatbelt tight and pulled out of the community bank parking lot. "Just like that! Rejected! How could they?" Zen knew he was losing his Midas touch and this was not the time to be doing so. The financial crisis had reached a boiling point and he still couldn't find any way to get the loan refinanced. Without immediate refinancing, the cost of servicing the debt would soon exceed the church's entire operating budget and Zen had already taken a sizeable cut in his pay to try to stem the outflow of money. The actual fact of the matter was that if he didn't get the loan refinanced immediately at a lower interest rate, the bank would undoubtedly call the loan. Zen knew that if that happened, there was no saving the church. The books were a mess. The capital campaign money had been used up long before the building had been completed and he had been running the church on a prayer and a song, literally, for the past six months. Things were dire and Zen was at a crossroads.

Breaking

Zen pushed himself away from the large round table where he, the bank loan officer, a retired bankruptcy lawyer and member of the congregation who was advising Zen pro bono, along with the entire finance committee had been meeting all morning. Zen heard them out with a mixture of incredulity and painful realization that he alone had created this mess. "Gentlemen, Ladies," he began, choking on the words as tears glistened at the corners of his eyes, "you have made your position known and as hard as it is to hear, I concede that it seems that we have come to a point where we must part ways. I never thought it would come to this, but if the only condition the bank has for refinancing the loan is my removal as the senior pastor, then it appears I have no choice but to leave."

As Zen spoke these words, thundering inside his mind was a muffled scream of anger. "This church is MY church! My church!" he thought defiantly. "They have no right! No right to take from me what I built with blood, sweat and tears." But inside Zen knew that he really didn't have a choice. Leaving was, sadly, the lesser of two evils. The other option was for the bank to seize the assets of the church, which mostly consisted of the building, sell it at auction for a fraction of what it was worth and recoup what they could on the remainder of the loan. This would have left the entire congregation without a place to worship and as much as he despised them for asking him to step down, he knew it was the only way. In that wretched moment, perhaps without even fully comprehending it, it ceased to be all about Zen. God was at work inside Zen, changing him forever.

The terms "mismanagement of church funds" rang in his ears and he knew deep inside that he had let everyone in the congregation, his family, his friends, the high net-worth individuals who had funded most of the capital campaign, himself and even God down. "Or maybe especially God," he thought to himself with an uncharacteristic moment of humility. "Maybe that was the whole problem. I didn't make this about God. I made it about me and I refused to see and deal with the financial chaos that was right in front of my face. I thought I could talk my out of this, the way I've talked myself out of every other tight spot I've ever been in." This realization stung deeply and a verse from Saint Paul's Letter to the Romans reverberated inside his troubled mind: "Do not think of yourself more highly than you ought, but rather think of yourself with sober judgment, in accordance with the measure of faith God has given you." "I wish I had and I wish I could," thought Zen, bitterly.

Zen wisely chose not to express these self-incriminating thoughts, excused himself from the room with as much dignity as he could muster, and proceeded to go to his office to box up his personal belongings. "I don't even get a week to say good-bye," he thought self-pityingly, but then added to himself, "I'm not so sure I want to see their faces when I tell them that I've run their beautiful church into the ground." Indeed, he did not want to do that and so he resolutely packed up several boxes of books, his robes, a few pictures and some wooden figurines of the nativity that a church member had given him last Christmas and carried them silently to his car. This was the end of an era and an end to the old Zen, this much he knew. He also knew that there was no way out of this mess. This self-imposed gaunt-let was one he must run through. There was no avoiding it. No smooth talking opt-out clause. He was in that moment, alone. Or, again, so he thought.

Regenerating
Zen sat in his car, staring out of the window of his SUV, eyes unseeing. He just couldn't go through with the agreed-upon plan that he start to attend Debtors Anonymous meetings at the local community center. His pride was already shattered. What did they expect him to do, grovel? Zen ground his teeth, clenched his fists and mustered just enough courage to get out of the car and walk down the path towards the unassuming double doors that led to the one of the meeting rooms in the commu-nity center. He was about five minutes late for the meeting, which didn't help, and he knew that all eyes would be on him as he walked in and found a seat. "Why did this have to be so damn hard," he inwardly complained. "You'd think that I was a derelict, a bum, a good-for-nothing, the way that I've been treated lately."

It was true, Zen's pride had taken a beating lately. To be sure, he still maintained a healthy dose of pride, albeit beaten down, battered and bruised, but he certainly wasn't his usually confident self. All was not lost, however, and for that small miracle, he was profoundly grateful. As it turned out, the ministry committee had found a way to salvage Zen's position as senior pastor of the church and still get the loan refinanced, but only on the condition that he regularly attend a twelve-step meeting for eighteen months and share his weekly learning, with a special mentor appointed by the local diocese. Attending the twelve-step meetings caused great shame to well up inside him every time he thought about them. They were the bitterest pills he had had to swallow during this entire process of righting the proverbial ship.

Worse still, he was required to confess his mismanagement of the church budget to the entire congregation during his next regular Sunday worship meetings, and humbly and contritely ask for their forgiveness. "Talk about tarring and feathering," he had complained at the time to a friend. "Christ, I'd rather be burned at the stake or live on the streets than deal with this crap." Zen's best side was definitely not being brought out by the growth plan that the ministry team had designed for him. He recognized that fact but felt helpless to do anything about it. He was bitter, resentful and angry. His pride had been deeply wounded and he knew it. But he also knew that they were right. He had issues he had to deal with, and deal with them he would, come hell or high water.

What felt like three years later, Zen congratulated himself on his six months of perfect attendance at DA and acknowledged that he really did feel better than he had in a long while. He still bristled inside, thinking of the self-righteous judgment coming from a few of the more pious members of his ministry team who always seemed so concerned about his rehabilitation. But even they did not spark his ire in nearly the same way, lately. For reasons unbeknownst to him, but feeling uncannily like the result of being touched by the Holy Spirit, Zen felt as if a huge boulder had been lifted off his shoulders over the past six months.

During the painfully slow process of the DA meetings he had started to uncover the bad financial habits and arrogant attitudes that had caused much, if not most, of his downfall. He had begun to recognize that under the guise of being a minister to others more needy than himself, he had actually been shoring up his own ego with praise and adulation from the congregation. It slowly dawned on him that the worship services were ministering to his needs more than theirs. Bottom line, he had serious narcissistic tendencies and they weren't pretty, but with God's help and Cecelia's support, he was in a much healthier place now.

"God *has* helped me," he thought reverently and humbly as he reminisced about the last six months. It wasn't as if he was "cured" or anything like that, but it was a huge relief to realize that he was redeemable, even with all the gross missteps that he had made over the past several years. And more amazing than that, the congregation still loved him. In fact, they had been more than gracious when he had gone through the personal hell of telling them about the state of the church's finances.

Their compassion had surprised him more than anything. "I guess the power of forgiveness really does come from above," he thought in real amazement as one by one, members of his congregation came up to him after that painful service and gave him a hug or looked him squarely in the face and told him that they still believed in him, still loved him and still prayed for him. "It's amazing grace," he said softly to himself as he got out of the car to walk down the now familiar walkway, through the newly welcoming and even friendly double doors of the community center and into the warm and non-judging ambiance of the DA group. "It's truly God's amazing grace."

Chapter Three

Emotional Regeneration

The Story of Lenny

Lenora Jeanette Bollingsworth, J.D., or "Lenny," as her friends, acquaintances and clients called her, was the top-performing senior partner with one of the largest corporate law firms in the northern metropolitan center where she lived and worked. A no-nonsense woman with all the warmth of a fire hydrant, Lenny wasn't exactly what you would call approachable, but she still had many proponents: business clients specializing in custom software design whom she helped navigate the choppy waters of breach of contract lawsuits. Aggressive opposing corporate counsel didn't faze Lenny in the least. In fact, she relished a good fight, especially when the rules of conduct were clear. She had been told in private by many of her partners that she had a chip on her shoulder the size of a baseball bat, a description she actually liked.

No one wanted to mess with Lenny. Standing 5'10" tall with a perfectly proportioned, model-thin body, she had what one could accurately describe as an imposing presence, especially for a woman, and she had been told more than once that she intimidated some of the young male lawyers in the firm. Her chic, close-cut curly hair framed a pretty face with wide-spaced eyes, high cheekbones and a sensual mouth that she downplayed as much as possible. Dressing in a no-nonsense professional manner, Lenny wore mostly gray and black pin-striped pantsuits with crisp white tailored shirts from Brooks Brothers and accessorized only with expensive leather pumps, a pearl necklace and a gold, diamond-rimmed Rolex watch. These were her only pieces of jewelry and she wore them every day, almost as if they were her good luck charms.

Lenny knew that she had the potential to look stunningly attractive if she had been willing to emphasize any of her more feminine attributes, or god forbid, wear a dress every now and again, but creating that kind of attraction for the benefit of the opposite sex held absolutely no appeal to her at all. In fact, more than once she thought that she simply wasn't genetically engineered to be in a relationship because the internal physical feelings she had read about people having when they fell in love had never happened to her, at least not in a way she would have recognized.

Lenny's cool demeanor and her complete disinterest in men meant she still maintained a bachelorette lifestyle at the age of thirty-nine. Finding a spouse and having kids had always been a low priority for her during her twenties and thirties and, being more than willing to give up nights, weekends and vacations for the sake of gaining promotions at the firm, she had had plenty of discretionary time to make senior partner at the relatively young age of thirty-six. Although Lenny sometimes thought that she wouldn't have minded being in a relationship now that she had made partner—as long as it was low maintenance, that is—she still didn't feel any burning need to be with anybody.

Various lawyers at the firm, both men and women, had invited her out for drinks or dinner after work, but she was always pre-armed with a valid and believable reason to say no. "It just isn't worth the effort," she thought to herself each time she passed on the opportunity to get to know one of her associates better. Indeed, Lenny had every reason to be reluctant to get to know others either in her firm or in the high-end condominium complex near work where she lived. Although she had divulged her family's dirty laundry to no one, Lenny had experienced what a therapist once told her was emotional abandonment and suffered from deep loneliness as the only child of an alcoholic father and a co-dependent, perfectionist mother. Thus, Lenny had grimly resolved to simply stay out of all messy interpersonal arrangements, like marriage, for the duration.

Each time she heard her parents fight as a child, Lenny would tunnel under the pink covers in her tiny bedroom with the paper-thin walls and make secret plans to escape to her own safe haven. Over the years, as Lenny grew older and had a chance to earn some spending money for a stereo and music collection, she had become adept at tuning her parents out by putting on earphones and listening to music as loud as she could stand it, so that no amount of verbal discord could make its way inside her cocoon of safety. She got so good at distracting herself that in her senior high school years, she found she didn't even notice if the conversation lagged at breakfast on any given morning after one of her father's particularly bad drinking binges the night before. For this respite she offered up profound thanks to whatever guardian beings from above were watching over her.

Not surprisingly, it was with a huge sense of relief that Lenny left for Western State College on a full academic scholarship when she was seventeen and even more relief when she found herself hired for three consecutive summers during college at firms with highly selective internship programs. After graduation she got a great job offer so she didn't really have to go home at all, except for a short weekend at the end of each year around the holidays to give her parents the obligatory visit and tell them, in non-specific terms, about her life. Lenny's parents were never violent or mean when she visited them; her dad simply self-medicated with booze continuously and her mom hyper-controlled everything to the point of total inflexibility. They were so completely out of touch with Lenny's experience of reality that she felt no desire to bring them up to speed, knowing it would be an unending project with very little upside.

Lenny knew her parents loved her in the best way they knew how, but she just couldn't stomach the tension at home when she would arrive and at first get fussed over by both parents and then ignored as her father proceeded to drink his Scotch whiskey and become belligerent or critical, and as her mother proceeded to pout or martyr herself by pretending to need to do all sorts of unnecessary household projects like refolding the linens in the bathroom closet.

Their modest house was always spotless and as nicely decorated as it could be with inexpensive furniture from the local thrift department store, but there was never any sense of peace there, and thus, in Lenny's mind, no reason to stay. So, she settled her pricking conscience by bringing them money when she visited at Christmas and sending a postcard from her solo vacations in the Bahamas every spring. She didn't want them to know that she went alone so she always wrote to them in glowing terms, describing all the things that "we did" at the beach, restaurant, casino, or bar. Of course she had never really told them who the "we" she referred to consisted of, and while they had probed at first, mercifully they never pushed the issue. That was part of the unspoken pact, she thought, "Don't ask, don't tell" sometimes was a good policy.

The only child of older African-American parents who had sacrificed a great deal so that she could go to college and then law school, Lenny had a fierce determination and a "don't mess with me" persona that made everyone want her as their lawyer but nobody want her as their friend. "It's just as well," she often thought to herself protectively. "Anybody who gets too close will always end up stabbing you in the back anyway. Why court disaster?" And that was how she went about her business, keeping herself a safe distance from well-meaning individuals, day in and day out, Monday through Friday, rain or shine, January through December. That is, until her fortieth birthday.

Waking Up

The snow was falling heavily outside and Lenny was alone on her fortieth birthday, which unfortunately fell at Christmastime: "Just when everybody is being most obnoxiously social," she thought morosely. This particular night, Lenny stood drinking a glass of expensive champagne in a fine crystal flute and watching the snow gently pile up on the streets and rooftops outside her third-floor picture window. The streetlights in the city twinkled brightly and colored Christmas lights hung on windows and doors here and there throughout the city, adding an especially festive accent to her view as she scanned the urban landscape. She had a fire burning in the fireplace, the lights were dimmed, and she had some Kenny G playing on the stereo system as she stood barefoot by the window, wearing only her silk pajamas and relishing the plush carpet beneath her bare feet.

But despite the obvious beauty apparent both inside and outside her window, Lenny felt a soul-searing loneliness and a deep sense of grief as she mentally reviewed the first forty years of her life. What had she really done with her life besides work, she thought despondently? Who would care if she was sick for a week with the flu or if she didn't show up for work because of a car accident? Who, that is, besides her secretary, who always knew where she was and the security guard whom she always tipped generously when she picked up her morning *Times*? These thoughts made her feel profoundly sad and deeply insignificant in a way that she had never been willing to feel before.

In this new universe of emotional vulnerability, Lenny was out of her element. This she knew for sure. And although she hated to admit it, she also knew that this situation needed to change. She had to surrender the absolute control she exerted over her entire life and emotions, risk being vulnerable and ask for some help soon, or she thought she might just curl up into an adult version of her childhood cocoon and never come out again. Unaccustomed as she was to these intense feelings,

Lenny felt frightened, another strange and unfamiliar feeling, and she started to wonder if suddenly, on the brink of her forties, she was going crazy. "Nonsense," she said firmly to herself. "I just need a vacation. It's been a long hard couple of months and I've done nothing but work." Despite this attempt at self-assurance, Lenny wasn't convinced that over-work was the only problem, but she still stayed up late that night searching the internet for a vacation that would allow her to get some rest and renewal. After deliberating for several hours, she finally chose a month-long meditation retreat being led at a holistic health center situated high above the rocky coastline of California, with a view that stretched across the vast Pacific Ocean to the horizon. Lenny went to sleep that night with a sense of hopeful anticipation about what was in store for her.

Breaking

A glorious blanket of springtime flowers covered the steep hillsides of Big Sur, California, unnoticed by Lenny, who wearily carried her suitcase into the sparsely furnished bedroom that was to be her private sanctuary during the month-long meditation retreat she had found online. Lenny wasn't into overt spirituality but she did recognize the need to be centered and grounded. She also wanted to see if she could be with her feelings for at least a little while without running away from them. She had never really allowed herself to feel fear and it disconcerted her.

Also, she had recently recognized a life-changing truth during the last few months of soul-searching and she need help understanding it. "I need to learn to be in a good relationship with myself before I'm ever going to be able to be in one with anyone else," she had unwillingly acknowledged one night as she remembered her birthday and her desire to crawl out of her skin to escape the feelings she was having. Even she knew the truism that you can't run away from yourself, no matter how far or how fast you run. The difference was that now she was ready, willing and hopefully able to stop running.

Lenny had been introduced to her meditation teacher when she arrived on site and he appeared to be a gentle giant, tall and lean with a shaved head and kind brown eyes. The thought of letting him get emotionally close to her didn't scare her too much. He didn't seem to be that dangerous, and besides, she trusted the look on his face. Over the years she had gotten very good at reading whether people were dangerous or not by the way they looked at her. It had stood her in good stead as a litigation attorney and now she would have to trust it to keep her safe as she went inward, into the dark, unswept corners of her mind and heart.

The first week of the retreat put Lenny into a state of relaxed and happy anticipation of what was to come. It really felt like a wonderful vacation; she ate incredibly fresh food grown in local gardens, got massages each day and spent her time walking along the cliffs and staring out across the vast expanse of ocean that lay just outside her cabin door. That was the first week, and Lenny had been warned that the retreat would get harder before it got easier.

This forecast unfortunately came true in the second week when Lenny started to feel a bit raw from all the unguarded conversations she was having with other retreat participants. Lenny didn't know exactly how to engage them without talking about work, but she had promised herself that she wouldn't think about the office for a month and she had made doubly sure that she couldn't use work as an excuse to escape by requesting full coverage from some of the junior partners at the firm during her time away. Thus, she would be forced to conclude that if she did end up compulsively checking her iPhone for emails, this would be just another means to run away from herself.

Each conversation that Lenny had felt like she was discovering how to share herself for the very first time. And then there were the days that were blocked off as silent retreat days, and on these days she sometimes felt as if she would cave into a black hole within herself if she couldn't find a way to escape from what she was feeling. Gratefully, after days like these she would seek out the guidance from some counselors on the premises who were prepared for just this kind of reawakening. One woman in particular named Tasha whom Lenny had gravitated to on the first week reassured her that this process of going within and discovering what she had been hiding from all these years was similar to what other participants were feeling and that the process was painful for everyone at times.

The reassurance that she wasn't abnormal helped out a little, but there were days when Lenny would rock back and forth on the rocking chairs set out on a wooden platform above the pounding ocean waves, watch the setting sun disappear under its blanket of dark water and yearn for an escape from the constant anxiety that dogged her. At times sleep blessed her with its presence and she drifted into a dreamless, restful repose that left her feeling refreshed and energized in the morning. At other times, she slept fitfully and awoke in a cold sweat, her mind racing with nightmares. Those were long nights and sometimes Lenny deeply regretted what she had gotten herself into when she made the decision to peel back the decades-thick layers of psychological armor with which she had surrounded herself, to discover who she was underneath. The regret never grew stronger than the slowly emerging sense of peace and trust in herself that was sprouting like a small seedling inside and she took this as a sign to keep going deeper. And deeper she went.

Regenerating

Being back in the office on the east coast, where spring had barely begun its long march towards summer, felt very strange after a month of dressing in sandals and loose flowing clothing, eating vegetarian fare, mediating and taking long walks along the edge of the sea. Lenny couldn't quite get her groove back for the first couple of weeks but then something inside of her kicked into gear and she remembered why she loved practicing law. She soon began to feel again the thrill of the hunt and the adrenaline rush that hit her when she devised a solid strategy with which to defend her clients.

Besides that thrilling and recognizable feeling, however, everything was different. Lenny got looks and smiles that she'd never gotten before and she actually returned them. She reached out to mentor some of the junior partners in the firm and help them handle the deluge of work they were always digging out from underneath. She returned the favor of an invitation to have dinner at her home after work to a couple of the partners down the hall who had extended offers to her to go out for drinks, offers which previously she had graciously, but firmly, declined each time.

Lenny felt a strange sense of exhilaration at the freedom she felt inside as she went about her business. The emerging lightness in her body and mind had erased years of stress from her face and the rigid way she used to hold her shoulders and neck had relaxed so visibly that she no longer broadcasted the "don't mess with me" message to the world. There were still nights when Lenny would lie on her back looking out of her big picture window at the familiar skyline and weep for the loss of her youth and all the friendships she never had, but these moments were always followed by an abiding and ever-expanding sense of gratitude as she turned her focus towards the future and what lay ahead of her.

Love and friendship which had once been meaningless words on a Hallmark card now seemed to be the two things she longed for most and she committed to herself that before the year was over, she would experience both. For that glimmer of hope on the horizon, Lenny felt immensely grateful and profoundly humble, two feelings that were also strange to her, but this time in a good way. Gratitude and humility now became her guiding attitudes and she practiced them daily, much to the amazement of her peers. At the end of one particularly rewarding day, she thought to herself quietly and courageously, "Maybe it's time to go home and reacquaint myself with the folks." And with that thought, she started to whistle and decided to cut the day short and go for a long walk along the river, hoping perhaps that she might bump into some stranger who would be her next new friend.

Chapter Four

Intellectual Regeneration

The Story of Penny

Penelope George, or "Penny" as she had been called since childhood because her auburn hair reminded her family of the color of a new penny, was the mother of three, director of volunteers for the United Way and a twice-published adult fiction writer. She was also a caretaker, a consummate hostess, and someone who provided the rudder whenever the winds of life blew a little too strongly for her children or her husband's liking. Penny's Indian-American heritage also meant that she had a deep respect for her husband Tom and for men in general and she tried, most of the time, to be respectful and kind when she was with him. She knew that he worked hard to provide a good living for the family and even though he wasn't overly demonstrative, she knew he loved her and never doubted his loyalty to her and their family for an instant.

Penny could have been taken straight from central casting in Hollywood, for she looked, acted and spoke like the prototypical "motherly type." She stood 5'4" and was plump, without being fat, with an inviting softness about her. She had her shiny, chestnut colored hair cut into a low-maintenance chin-length pageboy cut and she rarely wore makeup, nor did she adorn herself with any jewelry other than a simple gold wedding band and a watch her kids had given her for her birthday. Penny had never been into her looks, nor had they ever been something that she felt she was loved for, so the fact that she was starting to feel like a "middle-aged mom" and look a little drab to herself in the mirror really didn't bother her, except upon the rare occasion when she was going out with Tom to a cocktail party and felt frumpy, which is exactly what she was, she would remind herself pragmatically and then drop the subject.

Penny and Tom had been married for nineteen years in what Penny would have called a "marriage of friendship" if she had thought about it much, but she didn't really dwell on her marriage, nor on how happy or fulfilled she felt within it. It just "was what it was" and she saw no reason to spend precious time thinking about how it might have been, or could be, otherwise. Penny and Tom had three children: James, who was a sophomore in college, Hallie, a junior in high school, and Jenny, who was a thirty-year-old trapped in the body of an eighth grader. Penny never could figure out where her youngest child got her flair for fashion or advanced knowledge about boys and relationships, but she did pay special attention to Jenny's precociousness and often worried about Jenny getting into a serious relationship too fast.

Devoted, compassionate, resourceful and resilient were all words that had been used to describe Penny at some point or another and she certainly didn't lack for adoring friends or influential connections in the community. She ran a tight ship and her spacious, comfortable home in the suburbs was often a sane place of refuge for friends of her children who needed to escape from their own often emotionally turbulent homes. Penny had such a deep compassion for children and animals that her home usually resembled a small three-ring circus, with animals, kids, play rehearsals, blaring stereo music and dirty clothes all mixed up into a wonderful mélange of chaos. And in the midst of it all, Penny handled it with aplomb.

Like many deeply caring individuals, Penny paid a great deal more attention to meeting the needs of her family and friends than she did to her own basic needs like physical care and intellectual stimulation. In fact, she couldn't remember when she had last done something special for herself like a day at the spa for a massage and facial, or time spent reading a book that wasn't about parenting. She had promised herself at the beginning of the year that she was going to start walking each morning, sign up for a yoga class with her friend Helen and start attending Weight Watchers to get some help losing the extra twenty pounds that had managed to find its way, in an apparently permanent state, onto her petite waist and hips, successfully eliminating most of the more tailored outfits from her wardrobe. But despite these promises, she hadn't done anything to make a single one of them a reality.

Penny also felt a yearning to return to watercolor painting, something she had started to learn while in college and which she apparently had some talent for. She also longed for friends who weren't also on the "mommy-track," women who could speak to her about more than puberty, sports and teenage temper-tantrums. Penny had majored in math and biology in college and had a master's degree in public health. Despite this educational pedigree, she hadn't worked since her son James was born, almost twenty years ago now, not wanting to feel pulled between her desire to mother and her desire to work. There would always be time to get back into the world of work, she had told herself patiently when each of her three children were born, but a major transition back into the business world seemed to grow farther and farther away from her as she continued to invest in parenting and community involvement in a way that virtually assured that she wouldn't have time to collect her thoughts and figure out what to do next, professionally.

Despite the deep sense of satisfaction that Penny felt in her role as mother, she longed for an intellectual challenge, something she could really sink her teeth into. Penny often felt as if she were slowly stagnating in a world made up exclusively of moms and volunteers (not that they weren't also very accomplished but to her, their conversational topics lacked breadth and depth), with nowhere to turn for stimulation and peer-to-peer conversation on matters that extended further than the family circles she moved in and among.

Ironically, Penny had appropriately earned the admiration of many of her peers; she had risen to the top of the "mommy ladder" and her generosity, kindness and efficiency in all situations were considered a community resource. This public acknowledgement had gratified her for at least a decade, but now that Jenny was old enough to babysit and go out on dates, Penny felt less and less that her constant presence was critical to the wellbeing of her kids. In fact, Penny wasn't exactly sure these days if her presence was really critical to anything. This feeling caused her to feel a pit in the bottom of her stomach that got worse the more she thought about how redundant and unnecessary she felt these days.

Waking Up

Penny looked up from the law school application she was completing online. She had attempted this same application three times but each time she started to fill it out she gave up less than halfway through the daunting process, feeling that latching on to the idea of law school was simply a futile attempt to fill something inside her that couldn't be filled by another graduate degree. She knew she was intuitively right about this, but she didn't know why or what she should do about it. Tears of frustration stung her eyes as she leaned back in her chair and began to rub her neck thoughtfully. She knew that she longed to be working somewhere where she would be respected, fulfilled and challenged, but she had felt all those things for the past twenty years, why was it any different now?

"I really need to get a grip," thought Penny as she realized she had just run a red light on her way home from picking up Jenny from gymnastics practice. This was the third time this week that she had done something she half jokingly called brain-dead (even though she would have chastised her kids for using such unkind terminology). She found herself daydreaming a lot these days and wondering why her so-called perfect life was so unfulfilling. She felt bad about her lack of contentment and gratitude and for that reason kept her feelings to herself.

Tom had noticed that she hadn't been her usual cheerful self for the past year or so, but wrote it off to the symptoms of early menopause. They didn't talk enough on a really intimate level for Penny to feel comfortable bringing up her feelings with him, so her best friend Melinda was the only person who knew about her growing feelings of unrest and discontentment. Penny's three kids had been her primary focus for the past two decades and now she felt a little used up and disillusioned, despite the fact that her children were academically successful and socially quite well adjusted—"Everything a mother could want," she said to herself sadly.

"It would be nice if I felt the same way about myself as I do about my kids," she thought wryly, and then shrugged as she switched the radio over to hear the last part of one of her favorite Phil Collins songs. Something about his chronic wistfulness spoke to her right now and she wondered whether she needed to sign up for a women's retreat, or get a new haircut, or even do something more drastic like a little tummy tuck and some liposuction for her seemingly ever-expanding hips.

Penny had been an athlete herself, back in the day, a gymnast like Jenny. But she didn't feel much like one these days as she stood in front of her mirror every morning wondering where the extra padding of fat around her middle had come from. She realized that "middle age" had a firm grasp of her soul and was giving her pause, and a great deal of grist for self-reflection these days. She was barely into her forties and barring the unforeseen had plenty of good years left in her. She just wasn't sure what she wanted to be doing now that her primary focus on mothering was starting to become redundant and her kids were firmly grounded in their own identities and unique gifts and talents. "At least I've done a good job in that arena," she thought, giving herself some well-earned praise. "But what next, what next?"

Breaking
 Penny decided to give herself a weekend of solo reflection at the beach cottage that she and Tom had bought in their
first year of marriage. Actually "cottage" was a little too gener-
ous a term. It was more like a beach shack with its dilapidated
exterior of weathered gray shingles and the paint peeling along
the window frames. There was a double bed in one corner covered with an old quilt and pushed up against the window ledge
where a row of shells, sand dollars and starfish ran along it, col-
lected over the years by children and guests. In another corner
was a small square table with four wooden straight-backed
chairs, once painted a bright blue that had faded over the years
and now having a soft mottled appearance, which she found
quite soothing.

 There was an old mason jar with some old sea grasses in
it on the table and another window in the corner that looked out
across the sound. The third corner served as a makeshift kitchen
and had a small electric double burner for cooking coffee or
pancakes, a small fridge the size her son James had bought for
college, though decidedly older "and certainly less fresh-
smelling," she thought as she opened the door and smelled the
stale refrigerator air that had been trapped there for who knows
how long. There were some old plates and cups that had been
brought to the cottage over the years when they had grown too
worn or chipped to serve as everyday dinnerware at home and
a cup full of an assortment of spoons, forks and knives, none of
which matched another. The fourth corner had a small bathroom built into it with a toilet, small sink, even smaller mirror
and a narrow stand-up shower with a clear plastic shower curtain covered in blue cartoon fish and sea anemones. It had a
patina of grime which had become one with the plastic that
formed the prefabricated shower stall over the years and it
would not get clean, no matter how much elbow grease and
cleanser she applied to the project.

 Penny stood in the middle of the room, humming softly
as she looked around the room. It took a moment or two for her
to get reacquainted with the place. She hadn't been here since

Jenny was nine; usually, her kids retreated to the small shelter to get away from grown-ups, play guitar, drink beer and, she was sure, imbibe and ingest other less than legal substances. Penny grimaced a little as she thought of what teens would willingly put into their bodies to get a buzz, but felt at least somewhat mollified by the fact that allowing her kids free rein in the beach cottage had been a deal she had struck in return for a zero-tolerance policy of no drinking and driving. They had, as far as she knew, abided by this policy and for that she was grateful, as her mind briefly rested on the image in the newspaper last week of yet another youngster in their community who had been killed in a drunk driving accident.

Penny had told Tom and the kids that they were going to get a "mom-free" week and they could do whatever they wanted to, including staying up late and ordering take-out pizza, as long as everything was clean upon her return. Tom understood her need to get away and was actually relieved to discover that she had a plan for herself, because he had gotten quite concerned about her growing malaise but equally unsure about what to do to help her with it. Penny had excused herself from various coffee dates with her girlfriends and begged out of one meeting of United Way volunteers, and was actually amazed at how easily she could erase the events that she had previously considered so sacrosanct from her busy calendar. "Apparently I'm not actually as critical for the running of the planet as I thought," she teased herself and resolved to make a mental note that she wanted to resign from her role as director of the local United Way when she returned home. In fact, there were a number of things that she wanted to resign from, but that would wait. For now, she needed to go for a long walk to clear her head.

Penny took a light green windbreaker out of a small locker at the foot of the bed, wrapped a scarf around her head and stepped out into the windy salt air. The brisk cold stung her cheeks and she started to walk, realizing how much she had missed having time alone in the outdoors. Penny looked along the shore towards a distant lighthouse and resolved to walk in that direction until she felt like turning around, or hit the small crossroads grocery store, which was the closest thing to a town that existed in these parts. Penny walked and walked, thoughts swirling in her head.

First she did a mental scan of all the things that she had to be grateful for, a little trick she had borrowed from an Oprah show she had watched a year or two before. She mentally checked off each member of her family, her friends and her community involvement. Next, she gave thanks for her relatively comfortable lifestyle and her husband's career, which had allowed her to fund various household projects and let the kids participate in whatever sporting event or afterschool activity they exhibited any talent for.

Then she got into some harder assessments: her sense of play, for instance. "Where has that gone?" she wondered, remembering the cheerful, buoyant young woman she had been when she married Tom twenty years ago. She always seemed to be laughing then and she had lots of activities that brought her joy, including ballroom dancing, singing with a small community a cappella choir and spending time driving around the country roads near her home in the little second-hand Italian convertible Tom had bought for her as a wedding present. She remembered how she loved to listen to music and drive along, singing loudly and feeling totally free. She had actually felt that free when the children were young, too. "When was it that the feeling left me?" She shook her head as the years blurred together and any hope of finding a line of demarcation left her completely. "Oh well," she thought, "That was then and this is now. It doesn't really matter when it left me. What matters now is when it's going to come back."

Penny continued to do a mental accounting of her life and realized that she had neglected her personal sense of style as well. She never had been much of a *fashionista* but she had had a good figure and always dressed in a way that attracted men and made her feel pretty. "Pretty," she thought. That word hadn't been in her mind for along while, at least not in relationship to herself. "Hallie and Jenny fit that description, but not me. I really need to do something to feel more attractive. Maybe a makeover at the makeup counter at Nordstrom's?" she thought. This was an idea she admittedly had been having a lot lately but had continually dismissed as self-indulgent. "And my clothes make me feel like an old sack of potatoes," she continued in the same vein. "These stretchy fabrics with elastic waistbands make me feel like I'm always wearing pajamas. Nice pajamas, but pajamas just the same."

Tom had offered to take her out for a shopping spree for three years in a row on her birthday but she had always refused, saying that she wanted to lose weight first. "Well, that's not going to happen immediately," she thought realistically, "and I'm not getting any younger." With that, she resolved to let her husband take her out for that shopping spree, followed by a trip to Nordstrom's with her friend Belinda for a makeover, a new haircut at the local boutique where her hairdresser had been trying to update her style for months, and a date with the new physical trainer many of her friends were using at the local gym. That took care of the cosmetic issues which, while not inconsequential, were, she knew, not the real root of the problem. "Ah well," she comforted herself, "You've got to start somewhere."

Now her mental accounting took her to the harder issues: her mind and spirit. What had she done consciously to feed both in the past year? "No, forget the past year," she thought. "Make that the past ten years." It was true and she knew it. Her sense of apathy and discontentment had grown in direct proportion to her increasing involvement with the kids' activities and volunteering in the community. Not that those things weren't important, but they weren't everything. Penny paused as she had this thought and a light went on inside her head: "I made the kids 'my everything'! That's what I did. Nobody made me do this. I wasn't forced into servitude as a wife and mother. I freely accepted these roles and invested myself in them . . . but the problem is that I forgot the rest of me," she finished the thought for herself, soberly. This was actually the first time that Penny had realized that her own choices were the source of her problems, not her role as a mother, or wife or volunteer or anything else, for that matter. "It's certainly possible that I could have been just as discontent had I chosen to be a doctor or a lawyer," she mused to herself. "It would be exceptionally easy to let those roles define me as well."

This way of looking at things jolted her a bit. Penny hadn't expected to find that the problem with her life lay with the way she was looking at things. She really had thought that she needed a drastic change in all of her primary daily activities in order to "fix" her life. Now she realized that the answers to her struggles had been within her and she had refused (for whatever reason, but it didn't matter now what that reason was), to confront her own complicity in the matter.

As Penny continued to stroll down the shoreline, her breath started to catch and then she found herself crying softly and then more loudly, until the tears and the sobs came out in waves, like the waves beating upon the shore at her feet. "How did I miss this for so long? Here I was putting off my own life, thinking that my life was my role. My life is NOT a role. My life is whatever I happen to be doing right now, and right now my life is being a mess on the beach, crying and looking like something the seagull dragged in." Penny smiled at the silly image she had created by mixing her metaphors and weakly congratulated herself for at least not losing her sense of humor.

Penny stopped and stood looking out at the gray ocean, which had grown more menacing as she had been walking along, lost in thought. She hadn't noticed that a storm was brewing and if she didn't turn around now, she would find herself drenched and forced to walk in the driving rain all the way back. Penny turned around, but had only made it halfway home when the heavens opened. She was immediately soaked to the bone, despite the thin protective layer of her windbreaker. "No match for a summer thunderstorm," she thought and hopefully began to wonder if there were any old clothes left in the cottage that she could put on. She hadn't thought about getting caught in a rainstorm and just had shorts and t-shirts for what she had anticipated would be a sunny, warm relaxing time on the sand.

Regenerating

Penny started to run as the rain began to chill her and as she ran, she started to feel the buried energy that had been residing somewhere inside her cells start to burst forth with each step. She ran and ran and as she did, miraculously, she felt younger and younger, decidedly not "middle-aged" any more. She ran and felt stronger, not the victim of her "role" as a mother or wife or volunteer, nor the inevitable by-product of the inexorable aging process. She ran and she thought about the three books she had started writing that had lain unnoticed on the hard drive of her laptop. She ran and she thought about the boxes of colored pastel pencils and the watercolor paints and heavy paper that had been shoved onto one of the top shelves in the playroom closet. She ran and she remembered the collection of waltzes that she had bought on CD many winters ago so that she and Tom could practice dancing to them on cold Saturday nights and wondered where they could possibly have been stashed.

She ran and ran and she remembered and remembered and when she arrived back to the cottage, she was thoroughly drenched by the cold rain and out of breath but totally exhilarated by the physical challenge. All the possibilities she had started generating for her life quickened her spirit more than anything she had done or thought in recent or distant memory. Coming through the door and pulling off her sodden windbreaker, she fell onto the bed and started laughing.

The laughter started softly, just the way the crying had, and then began to slowly crescendo until she was laughing so hard that her stomach started hurting and tears sprang to her eyes. But this time, the tears were not tears of resignation but tears of joy, possibility and challenge. Penny gave herself a welcome home hug and started to strip off her wet clothes and head to the shower. As she passed by the little mirror in the bathroom she said, "Welcome home, friend." And with a small step, she slipped under the cascade of warm water and started to gently wash her now glowing body with tenderness and care, caressing every curve and loving every wrinkle. Penny had found her way back home.

Chapter Five

Physical Regeneration

The Story of Henny

Henrietta Maria Gonzalo, M.D., or "Dr. Henny" as she was fondly called by all her patients, was a pediatrician, mother of two and the beloved wife of Carlos Gonzalo, also a doctor, but one who had wisely specialized in one of the higher paying sub-specialties of cardiology. A wonderful and efficient physician, Dr. Henny had a brisk but soothing bedside manner honed by years of practice with her own kids, and there were not many situations that fazed her. Henny had married Carlos right out of college and amazingly, they now had two grown children of their own who had recently graduated as well.

Tessie, their twenty-three-year-old daughter, had already started her first year of medical school, and their twenty-five-year-old son Henry was still trying his hand at acting in New York City—and still struggling at it, he was the first to admit, with chagrin. She still hoped he would give up his dream to be an actor and go to law school because she knew it would be an easier life for him financially, but she never shared those thoughts with Henry, preferring to support him unconditionally because he might or might not come to those realizations on his own and she didn't want him to feel judged by her. Both the kids' work lives were stressful enough to preclude an early marriage for either of them and for this Henny was grateful, knowing first-hand how hard it was to be married during graduate school, with little or no money to ease the burden of keeping a home and raising kids.

At age forty-seven, Henny still had a well-maintained and nicely proportioned figure and she looked young for her age, which was gratifying. She had shiny, thick, lustrous black hair that she always wore tied up in a knot when she was at the clinic, but which she let down every now and again when she and Carlos went out for a nice dinner date. Carlos loved Henny's softer side and he was the only person she ever revealed it to. She felt very blessed to have a husband who was such a kind and gentle man and so good to her, allowing her to feel safe while showing her more vulnerable, feminine side to him. To the rest of the world, she was bulletproof and she liked it this way. Carlos balanced Henny and softened the parts of her that could get a little too businesslike. He had the heart of a romantic, which many thought was appropriate since he healed hearts for a living.

Waking Up

"Treat your body well. Otherwise, where will you live?" thought Henny rhetorically, as she sat upright on the examining room table and pulled the hospital gown the nurse had given her close around her shivering body. Then she got off the table and started to put on her clothes, slowly and thoughtfully. Never one to lose her cool, this time was no different than any other but the news that she had just heard wasn't exactly making her want to dance a jig either. After performing a routine physical exam, she and her primary care physician had just reviewed some MRI tests results, which had come out positive for MS.

"Well that would explain my blurry vision and difficulty focusing," thought Henny matter-of-factly. She also thought back over the dizzy spells she'd been having, accompanied by a general sense of fatigue and lethargy, symptoms she had even mentioned to Carlos with a little concern. This behavior was out of character for Henny, who almost never chose to mention the variety of physical aches and pains that she had been experiencing recently, preferring instead to maintain a stoic front on this subject. All these thoughts roiled around in her mind as she tried to square the doctor's orders that she would need to tend her body much more diligently and gently now, with her tendency to drive herself very hard, and to pay little attention to her own physical wellbeing. Accustomed as she was to having boundless stores of energy and being able to completely depend on her stalwart, trusty body to do what she told it to, the idea of coddling herself made Henny groan inwardly with distaste.

Henny had never openly acknowledged her own capacity for human frailty, even though she made a living healing other people's weaknesses. She had grown up with parents who both worked blue-collar maintenance jobs in the local hospital and were first-generation Americans from Mexico. They had blazed a path for Henny to follow and for this she was eternally grateful, knowing that many of her cousins still lived in poverty, over the border in Mexico.

Henny learned from both of her parents that self-reliance and hard work had figured heavily in the equation required to change their life circumstances. She honored them by being a good student all the way through school, consistently earning praise from her teachers by showcasing the internalized messages that she got every day about diligent, conscientious effort and plain old hard work. Henny secretly prided herself on her ability to get through medical school while starting a family and she would be the first to admit that her identity was closely tied to her strength and resilience. "Thus," she thought with frustration, "there is literally no room in my mind for accepting the identity of someone with a chronic, potentially debilitating illness like MS."

But resolute in her desire to always put a good spin on things, Henny visited several websites online to refresh what she knew about MS, because it wasn't something that she generally saw in her pediatric patients. She read that although the unpredictability of MS caused a great deal of anxiety, much research was being done on the subject and there were multiple new treatment options available for her, if ("not if, when," she added grimly to herself) she had a flare-up of symptoms. Henny believed in integrative medicine and the concept of mending the mind, body and spirit together, so she spent some time reading about holistic approaches to healing her body and resolved, regardless of its effect on the MS, to start eating a more plant-based diet and to consider getting a massage and even acupuncture on a regular basis to help relieve the stress on her body from this progressive disease. She also agreed with her doctor to start working three-quarter time by taking Fridays off so that she could slow down the pace of her life gradually and adjust to the different kind of lifestyle she could expect to have as someone living with MS.

Breaking

Just two days later, while she was working at the pediatric clinic, Henny started to feel faint on her feet, and to sway dizzily. She frantically clutched the counter, near where the rubber gloves, blood pressure cuff and box of tissues lay, and tried without success to regain her balance. A little boy sat on the examining room table watching her curiously, but said nothing. Henny felt her vision starting to blur and her feet and hands starting to tingle and then they went numb and she suddenly felt intensely weak, so weak in fact that she slid to the floor next to the cabinets, unable to stop herself despite her frantic efforts to hang on to the edges of the cabinet doors. She twisted herself around so that she could lie on her side but her head was lying against the base of the examining room table and she could just barely see her young patient sitting quietly on the paper covered table, shirt off, hands clenched quietly in his lap.

"Anthony," she whispered hoarsely with what little strength she could muster, "I need you to help me. Don't be scared, honey, I'll be fine. I just need you to get down from where you're sitting and walk down the hallway to the nurse's station and tell them that Dr. Henny needs some help. Will you do that for me?" she said, trying to steady her voice and sound calm, even though her heart was pounding in her chest and she could feel her body getting numb where it was pressed against the examining table pedestal. Anthony, who was only four years old, looked at her with his wide, brown eyes, not saying a word, and then slowly turned over onto his stomach and slid over the edge of the table and down to the floor, walked across to the door and stood on tiptoe to reach the handle.

Henny lay on the floor unable to move, while all kinds of morbid thoughts filled her mind and her body coursed with fear. After what seemed like an eternity, she heard voices and watched while two nurses and another staff doctor briskly entered the room and bent over her. She heard them asking her questions and pressing on parts of her body but she couldn't make a sound. She communicated fear through her eyes and then felt the soothing cool hands of her favorite nurse on her forehead and the calming tones of another one of the nurses reassuring her. Both of them were used to medical crises of this sort and their presence brought some measure of peace to Henny's anxious mind. Soon, she felt more hands touching her body and then she was gently lifted onto a stretcher and strapped in. One of the nurses pushed her while the staff doctor dictated orders to the other nurse who hurriedly scribbled down notes on a prescription pad.

"Apparently this is a real emergency," Henny thought, grateful that her collapse had occurred in a place crawling with medical personnel. She observed mutely while her co-workers transferred her to an ambulance, a medic attached a saline drip and checked her pulse, and the driver pulled out into busy traffic and headed towards the local hospital where Henny often visited her acutely ill pediatric patients. "Tables turning," she thought wryly. When they arrived at the emergency room entrance, the medics adroitly moved her out of the ambulance and into the hospital receiving area. Henny felt many familiar eyes looking at her with compassion and wondered what the other doctors were thinking as they watched their usually robust colleague being wheeled in on a stretcher.

Given her special status as one of the attending physicians at the hospital, Henny received VIP treatment and soon found herself in a private room at the end of one of the quiet floors of the hospital, and she gave a brief prayer of thanks for the little details, like privacy, that had been thought of and then efficiently handled by her nurses. Her husband Carlos arrived about twenty minutes later and strode purposefully over to her bedside and bent down to kiss her gently. He had been in surgery when he got the call that she had collapsed and had barely been able to control his anxiety as he completed the difficult procedure. Fortunately, he practiced in the same hospital where she had been admitted, so he didn't have far to go to get to Henny after he had finalized his portion of the surgery.

Carlos looked at Henny with love, tenderness and tears in his eyes and said to her, softly, "Sweetheart, it's time for a change of pace. I can't bear to lose you now, so you're just going to have to slow down and take it easy. I love you, baby . . ." The words caught in his throat as emotion surged past his professional demeanor and bedside manner, belying his very real concern for his beloved wife. Henny looked up at his concerned face and realized that he looked much older than she remembered him looking, an effect that was heightened by his intense concern for her. "Yes, I suppose I do," she conceded, "I suppose I do."

Regenerating

Several months later a refreshed and invigorated Dr. Henny strode to the front of a packed auditorium and stepped in front of the podium, adjusting the microphone downwards a bit to meet her. She looked out over the audience and noticed with gratitude that several of her female doctor friends were among the crowd. "Good for them," she thought, "I guess they've gotten the message that self-care isn't a discretionary activity anymore." After the obligatory introductions, Henny greeted her audience with the story of her collapse in the clinic; she followed it with a compelling profile of several women who were living with the bewildering array of symptoms that constitute the disease called MS and described the current research being done on the disease. This led into her primary message for women: "Regardless of whether you've been laid low by a disease such as MS, like me, or you're a 'perfectly healthy' middle-aged woman, like I used to be, you need to recognize that if you don't take care of your body now, you'll have nowhere to live."

After Henny's collapse and short hospital stay, she recuperated at home for several weeks and spent most of the time that she wasn't sleeping, researching intensive health care options for people with debilitating chronic illness. She expanded her search to include aggressive treatment options for people living with cancer and HIV-AIDS. During this time, Henny started to create in her mind the Gonzalo Wellness Institute for Women dedicated to "the pursuit of toxicity-free living." She had always been a follower of holistic methods of healing, in a superficial sort of way, but this time the energy, drive and motivation to create a place of wellness for women became a burning passion.

Henny had the zeal of a religious convert and spent the hours that she allotted for work (which were now half of what she had previously worked) either reading, writing or lecturing on the subject. In the hours that she kept for her own rehabilitative therapy, Henny explored the many forms of non-invasive holistic healing available to her. Included in her list were meditation, tai chi, yoga, massage and acupuncture. She performed a comprehensive review of most of the Eastern and Western healing methods in current use and elected to start meditating each morning and to experiment with acupuncture, which she had heard great things about. With her husband Carlos as her biggest supporter, she also agreed to co-deliver a keynote speech with him at the upcoming National Multiple Sclerosis Society conference drawn from a new book that she had begun to write called *Where Will You Live?* based on her personal story of MS. "I actually believe that this story will have a happy ending," thought Henny as she proceeded to undress for her twice-weekly massage. "Or at the very least, I will be happy *while* it is ending," she added philosophically and climbed onto the massage table, relaxing in the warm, lavender-scented room and happily anticipating what was to follow.

Part Two

Shining Stars

*Although the world is full of suffering,
it is full also of the overcoming of it.*

Helen Keller (1880–1968)

Introduction

Alchemy and Transformation

*Alchemy: any magical power or process of
transmuting a common substance, usually of little value,
into a substance of great value.*

What follows are stories of alchemical transformation. In
Part Two, the characters who regenerated their broken parts in
Part One have grown into people who have chosen to trans-
mute their brokenness and subsequent regeneration into great
value for the world. Each individual's alchemical process takes
the tragedy and suffering of life and turns it into an original life-
giving creation of their own mind and heart. Each of them
resolve, with a passion born of their own suffering, to help heal
the suffering of others by writing, teaching, connecting, mentoring and speaking out about their own stories in order to help
the people they touch to grow.

The transformation in each of these stories takes individuals whose lives have had an already considerable impact on
the people in their families, hometowns, and workplaces and
raises it exponentially so that it impacts individuals on a
national stage. The word transformation describes not just a
change in degree, but a change in kind. The process of moving
beyond regeneration into alchemy and transformation requires
unending persistence, even when the initial work of healing has

been successfully concluded. In this way, shattered stars go on to become shimmering stars whose love-light fills the lives of everyone they meet. They have taken their contributions out of the realm of the personal and into the realm of humanity as a whole. When individuals start to operate on this most transcendent of levels, a huge sea change in the way the world works can be expected. This new way of being allows these transformed individuals to channel their newfound strength, wisdom, resiliency and compassion out into the world's atmosphere, touching and healing on a huge scale.

History tells of great individuals whose lives have reached this pinnacle of true service to the world: Gandhi, Mother Teresa, Martin Luther King, Jr., and many others have gotten to a place where their leadership and their very presence transforms the most ordinary and mundane aspects of life into gold. This gold shows up as stories of healing, hope and redemption in the individual lives of the people they touch, lead, exhort, pray over and heal. And throughout the process of touching and healing, they continue to learn about themselves and to file off the rough edges in their own lives that always emerge because of their own fundamental humanness.

In the following stories, each individual sets a rippling wave of transformation in motion and then continues to stir the water to send wave after wave of positive energy out after it. The ripple effects of transformed leaders, those brave souls who have gone through the process of being shattered and emerged as shining stars, never stop. They go on and on, like a legacy of love that gets passed down through generations. This kind of transformation never ceases to transform others and never ends, itself. It is borne of humility and love, wisdom and courage, generosity and joy. Come and meet the shining stars.

Chapter Six

Spiritual Alchemy

Ten's Transformation

Ten hung up the phone and chuckled softly. "Who would have thought that I would go from running a global pharmaceutical company to speaking on the Dr. Phil show?" Ludicrous as it sounded, it was true. Several months earlier, Ten had published a book about Paul's suicide called *No Light in the Darkness* and his publicist had insisted he send a signed copy to Dr. Phil. The publicist felt it carried a poignant message to other parents and one that he believed Dr. Phil would be likely to endorse. Ten had laughed at the idea but agreed to sign a copy, just on the off chance that his publicist was right. The incident had slipped his mind until just now, when his publicist had called to tell him that he had been invited to appear as a special guest on the Dr. Phil show.

Ironically, although Ten had once been a very self-assured individual, always ready, willing and able to speak in front of any number of people on the many subjects that interested him, he now felt an uncharacteristic wave of anxiety flood him with nervous energy as he contemplated speaking on a nationally syndicated television show seen by millions of viewers. Ten's pride had been knocked out from under him, like a knight's horse in a jousting match. Now, his personal awareness had increased sufficiently for him to realize it was hubris that had created the wall of separation from Paul and this realization had gouged a deep, painful wound of regret that festered incessantly within his soul. The old adage "Pride goeth before a fall" had certainly been true in his case and he now spoke earnestly and often on the subject of what he chose to call "humble parenting," which he advised parents to actively practice all the way through their kids' late teen years and into the early twenties. He admonished parents not to let their teenage children struggle to figure life out on their own, just because they might believe or even look as if they can. "They're really still kids who need guidance, love and support at every age, but especially in their teen years," he would say, often choking back emotion. His stories hit home and he knew it. He strove to change the way parents related with their children by touching their own broken hearts with his.

Ten's life had changed dramatically since Paul died. He had undertaken a radical accounting of every aspect of his life in an effort to find out where he had gone wrong. He spent time in counseling to get help from an objective third party so that he wouldn't descend into despair or self-pity. He reached out to other parents who had suffered the death of a child and spoke to support groups about his experience, letting them see the once proud and pristine man, now humbled and reflective. Ten also invested time in very difficult conversations with each member of his family. He asked Susan what she needed in order to feel loved, supported and cherished. He also humbly let her know that he needed her, too, an admission he would never have made in an earlier time.

Ten's daughter Mariel had gone through a deep period of grief when her brother died, and she carried the scars of anger that had no outlet until Ten gave her hours of his time, going for long walks, listening to her, genuinely hearing her fears for perhaps the first time, and likewise telling her his deepest thoughts and feelings, hoping that she would learn to trust him again. At first, Mariel rebuffed his repeated overtures, but over time, she tentatively let him hear what she had been feeling since Paul's death. It broke his heart to hear her pain, but made him eternally grateful that he hadn't neglected her as long as he had Paul.

Ten also held out his hand in friendship to his stepsons, Nathaniel and Pete, letting them know that he wanted to be a part of their lives and asking them if they would be willing to include him. He now knew better than to preach, but he offered his support to help them with their life decisions going forward. They were both cool and non-committal initially, but little by little warmed to him as they noticed the time and attention he was giving to their mother. He knew all too well that actions speak louder than words, especially to teenagers, so he didn't push, but rather waited gently for their attitudes towards him to shift. Slowly, but surely, they too gave him their trust and shared their honest feelings in a more forthcoming way.

Each of these conversations changed Ten in ways that he could not have predicted. While each conversation made him feel older, wiser and a little sadder, he also felt gentler and less fragile inside. It was as if sharing the pain as a family strengthened the torn fabric of each of their individual lives. Each time another bond was reconnected, he breathed more peacefully. Each time he realized that he had another chance he felt overwhelming gratitude for the opportunity to make things better. And each time he spoke to a parent who was struggling with a child, he looked deeply into their eyes with compassion, listening quietly to their story, letting them know that he didn't judge them, that he understood their struggles, and that he wanted to help them find a way to forge the turbulent river that separated them from their children.

And on a day much like any other, Ten stood in front of the mirror, shaving. He remembered, as he did almost every day, that he stood in this exact place that morning years ago when he received the phone call that shook the very foundations of his world. The grief he had carried within his heart since Paul's death had become a constant companion, which had morphed over time from a black hole of anguish to the omnipresent bittersweet presence of memories. He still could not comprehend the point of Paul's death at such an early age and in such a violent way, but his impassioned outreach to troubled parents across the nation helped him believe that Paul had not died in vain; his life had not been wasted.

Ten slowly came out of his reverie and looked into the weary eyes staring back at him in the mirror. He gently ran his fingers through his hair, stroked the rugged lines etched on his face and felt a deep sense of peace. He knew that his once rugged good looks had been exchanged for the emotional scars on his face that he bore from the wound in his heart. And his once troubled heart was now filled with the spiritual serenity of a soul regenerated and ready to serve his life's purpose: to make the life of his son Paul replete with meaning and value for the world. He knew for sure that with the love and support of others, he had made it so and would continue to do so as long as he lived.

Chapter Seven

Material Alchemy

Zen's Transformation

Zen looked again with delight at his electronic bank balance on the computer screen, happy to see the accumulating zeros in front of the decimal point. After a year of regular attendance at DA meetings, Zen had publicly declared his commitment to help others whose lives had been blighted by financial chaos, through the creation of a financial literacy project he wanted to start at the church, funded entirely out of his personal income. Zen figured that if he started teaching his congregation about finances and helped them avoid the temptations inherent in over- and under-focusing on money he might have as much, if not more, of an impact on the hearts and lives of the people in his church as he did through his sermons.

Zen wanted to teach this in a creative way, just to keep the heaviness of the subject from weighing people down. In the service of this objective, he decided to have an off-site training for his Sunday school volunteers, which focused on teaching positive money habits for all ages, from five-year-olds to fifty-five-year-olds. He invited and inspired additional volunteers to teach this age-appropriate material to the Sunday school teachers with the intention of creating a money school, which would throw a completely new twist into the usual Sunday morning curriculum.

During the past year, Zen had made a concerted effort to read everything he could about financial stewardship, investing, saving, and budgeting to live within one's means. He now felt a genuine calling to serve others through a practical ministry that was built upon his very personal failure. It was as if God used his weakness much more effectively than He had ever been able to use Zen's considerable charisma.

In fact, Zen was more real, more genuine now than ever before. He still had the same strong presence, the same infectious energy and the same enthusiastic, passionate preaching style that engaged hearts wherever they were in their spiritual journey. However, it was his failure, his admitted weakness, that people could really relate to. His new focus gave his ministry a vitality and authenticity that brought searching souls from all over the community to worship, hoping to find some peace there. Now the church was growing, but not because of Zen's personal power, but because of his personal failure. The irony of that fact was not lost on Zen and it made him laugh at God's contrary sense of humor. "Every valley shall be exalted, and every mountain and hill shall be made low: and the crooked shall be made straight, and the rough places plain." He thought of the words from Isaiah and realized that he had been made both low and plain, and for a very good reason.

Zen had enhanced his personal financial literacy after he realized what a negative impact his ignorance and cavalier attitude towards money had created in his own life. Although he felt foolish for such a fall from grace, he now was passionate about giving help to others in his congregation with the same challenges. With genuine credibility borne from the wounds of his own failure, he helped members confront their own money demons and learn about themselves in the process.

Surprisingly, several of the wealthier members of his congregation were eager to participate in this program and offered to share about their own habits of financial stewardship. Thus, God leveraged the diversity of the congregation and members who had no official role in the church community into instruments of His peace, in and amongst Zen's congregation. What had started as a sideline activity for Zen became a focal point for the church's community ministry, both within and outside of the church walls, as the word spread and members invited their friends to join in. When people learned God's word could be so practical and help with such material concerns, their hearts were opened to learn of His love. God was now working through Zen in a way he never imagined.

Zen kicked off the start of his money school from the pulpit one Sunday with his own story of brokenness and regeneration. He ended with this exhortation: "I have made a commitment to God, myself and all of you that I will continue my process of recovery with respect to money. And now I want to challenge you to make a commitment to yourselves and each other. I want you to form small groups of four to six, select one of you to be a host, and gather together at your homes each month to speak openly and honestly about your challenges with financial stewardship and how you can live and give generously from a place of abundance. From those unto whom much has been given, much will be required. While I have been embarrassed, broken, shamed and laid low, God has given me grace, peace and plenty. He has given me the precious gift of redemption and He offers that to you. Not just in your finances, but in your very soul."

At the end of the service that day, Zen hung out in front of the church to chat with members of his congregation. The post-service energy of the crowd around him swirled and buzzed and the sound of intense conversation on the subject of financial literacy filled him with a sense of deep satisfaction: not in himself, but satisfaction in serving a great God who heals all brokenness in the lives of those who wait for Him. Zen knew that God was leading him now to serve with his full energy, passion and commitment but with a newfound humility that caused his message to be even more powerful and pertinent than ever before. He felt humbled, yes, but newly made whole, in a state of regenerated peace and serenity, with nowhere to go and no place to be but precisely where he was. "Grow where you're planted," he thought with a smile. And that's exactly what he intended to do.

Chapter Eight

Emotional Alchemy

Lenny's Transformation

Lenny sat absentmindedly twirling a spoon in her coffee cup with her right hand while her left provided a convenient resting place for her chin. From her perch at one of the café tables in the office break room, she stared out into the snow-covered city streets and contemplated how to establish the new mentoring program that she wanted to build for junior associates at her law firm. She had been musing about creating a meaningful new offering, one that could become a truly unique connection between her colleagues, focused on kindness and mutual respect rather than on competition and zero-sum scenarios. She thought of calling it "Face to Face."

In the months following her therapeutic visit to Big Sur, Lenny had often reflected on the powerful source of her transformative experience. In her mind, it all had started when she felt truly seen during that retreat. Thinking back on the experience, she still had difficulty articulating, even to herself, the nearly inexpressible positive feelings of validation she had gotten during meetings with her counselor. She could still recall the intense emotions she felt when she experienced the steady gaze of her counselor, quietly seeing her with non-judging compassion as she wept and shared her pain, regrets and insecurities.

Now that she was back on *terra firma*, in the old familiar setting of her law office, she wanted to create a way to replicate this liberating experience in her business setting. She knew that there was no better way to foster relationships between people, to break through their petty differences, and to genuinely seek and find understanding, than by looking into the eyes of another. Her counselor had seen through her eyes and straight into the depths of her hidden soul and that experience had been one of the greatest gifts she'd ever received. It had forever changed the way she thought about interpersonal interactions. "If I can get the lawyers at our firm to really see each other, then maybe in time, our clients will follow suit." It was a stretch, for sure, but one that Lenny was more than willing to attempt.

Truthfully, Lenny now felt a higher calling than just winning at litigation, and hence her prodigious energy and intellect needed a place to be channeled. She wanted to give back and pay it forward, by bringing care and compassion into her circle of influence. Somewhere in her spirit, she felt called to encourage her colleagues to see people as people, not merely as clients, defendants, plaintiffs or "opposing counsel." Lenny wasn't naïve, she had learned the hard way that the legal profession spawned adversarial gamesmanship, fostered aggression and manipulation for advantage, but she also knew that she felt ready to take it all on. In point of fact, she was compelled to try; creating Face to Face was now something she had to do.

Lenny's first move was to meet with the senior partners and sell them on her idea. She couldn't do this alone; she would need at least a couple other experienced lawyers who were willing to mentor young lawyers to learn a more collaborative, less adversarial style of litigating. Lenny hoped that together they could inspire the other senior partners to become allies, helping her to bring this model of interacting into the world of business law.

Lenny knew in her heart that this could be an antidote to the general trend in law of promoting the aggressive zero-sum game of "attack and protect" that she had learned and practiced all of her life. She knew that it would be a tough sell to the young lawyers because the idea was so radical but still, she thought it was worth giving it a shot. Lenny had recently become friends with Jake and Catherine, two lawyers who were both senior partners in the firm and had been around a long time, but hadn't gotten to know Lenny until recently. She thought they would be good candidates to start the project with her and excitedly shared her ideas with them, watching hopefully to see what their reaction would be to this innovative idea. To her surprise, they were more than willing to start a small pilot program with her and create a loosely structured curriculum to follow. Now that she was on a roll, Lenny felt relatively certain that some of the young lawyers who were struggling with the cutthroat nature of the business would be more than happy to participate in this learning process with her, especially now that she had gained a certain level of popularity with them.

Lenny had returned from California a different person, one who allowed her humanity to show, and her new vulnerability and openness had not gone unnoticed. Lenny had probably heard most of the lawyer jokes floating around at cocktail parties, and she had to admit, she used to resemble some of them. Now despite the commonly held assumptions about the selfish, back-stabbing, unscrupulous nature of most members of the legal profession, she was ready to chop her way through the kudzu of bad karma that she and others had created for her profession and create a new model for the practice of law, one that allowed for heart and head to coexist, where a passion for the law and a passion for justice could coexist with a passion for her fellow humans. This new spin brought nobility to her calling to serve in this profession and she yearned to inspire others to eliminate the bad and co-create the good.

As Lenny completed explaining her plan to Jake and Catherine, she marveled at their positive reaction. They were not merely lukewarm in their receptivity, which was all that Lenny had dared to hope for; they were in fact on fire about the idea. Her two new friends not only wanted to meet her for a glass of wine casually after work, but also wanted to invest in co-creating Face to Face with her. She was thrilled, but also filled with trepidation. Despite her driving passions, this foray into the softer side of interpersonal relationships was more than a bit unsettling for her and she wanted to be sure that they were really invested before she got too far into the design with them.

The project was ambitious on many levels. First, it would require a significant commitment of time to design the teaching material. Second, it would require some political maneuvering to get it sanctioned by the other senior partners as a valid way to approach litigation. Third, it would require a great deal of discretionary time (which meant weekend time, given their long work hours) from all three of them, as they worked together, thinking about the context in which the new skills would be used, and how to best engage their students. But Jake and Catherine appeared excited and more than willing to try the idea, and so was Lenny, so they agreed to meet the following weekend for a day of work at Lenny's office to see what they could produce.

It was late Saturday night when Jake, Catherine and Lenny finally put the finishing touches on their mentoring curriculum. They had spent the entire day creating teaching collateral and designing role-playing scenarios that would challenge their students, from every imaginable angle and a few unimaginable ones, just to keep them on their toes. Now, they were tired, dead tired–but tired in a fulfilled, complete way rather than an exhausted, depleted way. An empty pizza box and a couple of mostly empty bottles of wine sat on the desk in Lenny's office. Shoes and sweaters lay strewn on the floor where they had been kicked, as each of them got a little more comfortable and settled in for the long haul ahead of them. The whiteboard was covered in scrawl, bringing believable characters into existence, creating complex business contexts, setting up opposing, emotionally charged issues and adding ambiguity, just to make their improvisational skits ultra-challenging. Once

the teaching points had been identified, they had tested these
skits out themselves, each of them trying on all the roles: plain-
tiff, defendant, and the legal defense team for both sides. It had
been grueling.

It had been a blast spending the day together and Lenny
felt intellectually invigorated. More importantly, she felt emotionally close to her collaborators. Even though there were still
a great many things she didn't know about them or their personal lives, during the process of designing the mentoring program, questions about families, life paths, special friends, major
failures and significant successes peppered the conversation and
were answered with candid forthrightness. Lenny even felt
strangely comfortable sharing about herself and her childhood
with them. She told them about her trip to California and the
process of watching the ocean and crying about her loneliness.
Why she was sharing these intimate pieces of her recent past
she could not answer. She only knew that the more she trusted
her friends, and they more they shared with her and she with
them, the lighter she felt. This feeling exhilarated her in a way
that felt warm and enlivening, without any residual anxiety
attendant to any of these uncharacteristically vulnerable self-
revelations.

It was close to midnight when Lenny turned to her
friends and reached her arms out to them for a football-style
huddle. They were all more than a little bit tipsy, so this completely un-lawyer-like behavior seemed totally appropriate and
fitting. They put their heads together like cows sheltering from
a snowstorm and Lenny shared with them, in tentative but
earnest tones, about how deeply she appreciated their friendship. Jake and Catherine were a little taken aback by this emotional sharing from the formerly fearsome Lenny, but they
followed her lead and both, in turn, echoed her sentiments.
Finally, all three committed to deepening their friendship on
the following Saturday, when they were going to hold their first
Face to Face mentoring day with the junior legal staff.

Thankfully, and gratifyingly, when Lenny had pinned a sign-up sheet on the bulletin board in the break room it had filled quickly so they didn't have to suffer the embarrassment of working in an almost empty meeting room. She noted with satisfaction that the names were not just the usual suspects: the perfectionist, hyper-competent types who were always looking for ways to earn brownie points with the senior partners. In fact, she saw the names of two junior partners who had never spoken a word to her and she knew they had often watched her walk the halls with a guarded silence that had once closely resembled her own. It was satisfying to see that there were others at the firm who, like her "old" self, had spent their lives observing others from the safety of their brilliant and well-defended legal minds. For reasons that she couldn't know, they had decided to cautiously step out of their protected fortresses and share in the mentoring process. Lenny thought to herself that she would not have been so bold had she been in their shoes, and then smiled, relishing the idea of reaching out to them and bringing them into the warm camaraderie of what she had started to fondly call the Face to Face Family.

The following Saturday arrived before they knew it and Lenny, Jake and Catherine met early for a coffee at a Starbucks in the building lobby and then filed into the elevator to ride to the eleventh floor offices and get set up for a full day of teaching. All three were in incongruently high spirits, especially since they were working on a Saturday. The energy and laughter that filled the meeting room would have been appropriate for a wine and cheese party to celebrate a legal victory, perhaps, but hardly the sort of emotions you'd find at a workshop for young lawyers on how to engage in authentic, collaborative dialogue. The "inappropriateness" of their levity didn't bother them in the least and they bantered and joked as they greeted each of the ten participants with their own plastic lei and a grass skirt.

They had decided to make the entire experience so playful from the start that the young lawyers would take it as a sign to loosen up and let their creativity and ingenuity flow, rather

than standing on ceremony, which would have been their
default behavior. When the last associate walked in the door,
Lenny greeted her with a pink lei and fluorescent green grass
skirt and then whispered in her ear that she was going to be the
first "guinea pig" for the skits. Lenny felt a thrill of excitement
run up her spine as she called for three more volunteers, set the
context and prepared her young recruits to think about how
they would approach the faux legal battle they were about to
engage in.

She smiled a huge smile and glanced across to see Jake
and Catherine watching her. She had created a learning community of like-minded individuals and not once had she
stopped to think about whether she should be open and free in
her self-expression. Lenny had blossomed into a new way of
being. She was finally at home in her own skin and it was intox-
icatingly wonderful. At that moment, she knew why. She had
come Face to Face with herself and as a result had a deeper
appreciation of and loving tolerance for whom she was and
whom she wasn't. Big Sur had been a moment of truth and that
truth had set her free.

Chapter Nine

Intellectual Alchemy

Penny's Transformation

Penny stopped her bicycle, pulled it up onto the side-walk and walked slowly past the For Sale sign in the front yard of the slightly dilapidated old Victorian house that stood, empty and forlorn, at the end of Main Street. Penny had been by this house more times than she could possibly count, but she'd never noticed it before, not really noticed it. For some reason, the old house beckoned to her from her perch on the bicycle seat that sunny September day and called to her to come and explore. So, here she was, wandering around the side, then the back and then the other side of the big old building and up onto the wraparound porch which covered the front and two sides of the centenarian structure.

She walked tentatively towards the heavy oak door with the oval-cut glass window and peered inside. She could see an inner vestibule and a second door and then what looked like an open area that was the landing for the grand staircase that wound its way down the left side of the house. If she squinted, she could barely make out a long hallway that ran down the center of the house and then her view faded into the darkness.

Penny stood on the porch, looking at the fluted columns that supported the porch ceiling and out into the tangled patch of weeds and blown-out dandelions that once boasted a garden. It was early autumn and the graceful old maple tree that stood majestically sheltering the porch had just started to reveal the faintest blush of orange on the tips of some of the leaves. A soft wind blew a few strands of hair into her face and as she brushed them away, she felt a tear on her cheek. "Why am I crying?" she thought, a trifle impatiently. For the life of her, she didn't know why, but the tears were coming fast and heavy now and rolling down her face onto her blue cotton jersey and old blue jeans. "I've really got to pull myself together," she thought, and with that, she sat down on the front steps of the porch and pondered her seemingly inexplicable emotions.

As Penny thought, the image of an old house, well cared for and brightly painted, with soft incandescent lighting glowing through the tall, gracious windows, crossed her mind. She imagined walking inside and seeing each room teeming with activity. In the front parlor stood three easels and three contented women, about Penny's age, in smocks with their hair pinned up and paintbrushes in their hands, listening to Mozart's *Eine Kleine Nachtmusik* and painting their individual versions of paradise. A fire's glowing embers filled the far corner with light and warmth and the soft saffron yellow of the room glowed even more warmly with the addition of the firelight.

She walked through the front parlor into the middle parlor and there she saw a group of six women who were learning how to quilt. They all had a piece of the quilt and were working on their stitches, with their fabric pulled taut inside the quilting hoops, quietly talking and sharing stories about their days, their children and their longings. The soft rose color of the walls in this room warmed their complexions and they all looked young and peaceful. In this room, Penny imagined that she heard Pachelbel's famous canon providing a soft accompaniment to their quiet artistic pursuit.

Penny reluctantly brought herself out of her daydream reverie and back to the spot where she was sitting on the hard boards of the porch floor. The tears on her face had now dried and she felt a warm surge of energy flow through her body as she excitedly bounced down the steps, climbed on her bicycle and started to ride home. She knew now why she had been crying. Her daydream fantasy of this house wasn't new. She had been having little snippets of this dream for years and always had wondered what they meant. This old house triggered that memory once again, but this time with form, substance and three-dimensional clarity. It was all at once quite real.

She had always loved this particular dream when it would visit her, from time to time, throughout the years. It had often filled her with a sense of inexplicable peace; peace that she had rarely felt in those days. Now, her peaceful emotions enveloped her tired spirit, just as the old wraparound porch enveloped the tired house, and she realized that those former days were converging into this very moment, when a ramshackle old house finally brought substance to her dreams. At last, all of the pieces fit together and she realized that her old dream could actually define her new purpose: she would create a space for women to express themselves through art, reconnect with their creative energy and become whole again, renewed and regenerated through the creative process.

Penny pedaled home as fast as she could, parked her bike in the garage and bounded, a little breathlessly, into the house, her forehead damp with beads of perspiration and her auburn hair sticking to her face where the bicycle helmet had held it close. She impatiently poked her head into every room calling out loud for her husband, Tom, whom she knew was puttering around somewhere on one of his numerous house projects. She finally found him in the basement creating something with wood and glue but she didn't stop to ask what it was. Instead she blurted out her story of finding the old house. "Tom, I found it! It's perfect and it just needs some love and attention and a little elbow grease and some paint and a few repairs here and there and maybe a new window pane or two but it's just perfect." Penny paused to take a breath and Tom started to laugh at her childlike enthusiasm. He loved seeing his wife happy again and now she seemed to positively radiate with glowing delight, fueled by her new purpose.

"Well, let's go get a glass of lemonade and you can tell me all about it," he said. Tom's warm, familiar voice stirred Penny's emotions and she felt herself melt inside as he reached out for her hand. She hadn't had intimate feelings for Tom in at least a decade but suddenly, seemingly out of nowhere, she started to feel an old familiar surge of warmth and passion fill her body with coursing energy and she could feel her hand trembling in his.

They climbed the basement stairs, which opened into the sunny, lived-in kitchen, and Penny went to the fridge and pulled out a glass pitcher of ice-cold lemonade that she had made for the kids to have after school. She poured two glass tumblers full of the pale yellow drink and added to each glass a mint leaf that she had picked that morning from the garden. They sat down together at the kitchen table with a few pieces of paper and some crayons that Penny had found in a drawer under the counter, shoved there after one of the kids' innumerable social studies projects.

Tom listened intently as Penny began to sketch her vision quickly and talk about her daydream on the porch of the old house. "It's perfect for my women's creativity center, honey! There's so much space there that we could have any number of activities going on at one time. There's a big kitchen for clean-up and for messy things like working with clay or washing out paintbrushes and enough elbow room so nobody has to feel cramped.

"We could fill each room with different art materials and have women work with whatever medium the spirit moved them to choose on any given day. We could have music playing and there would be quiet rooms for women who just wanted to sit quietly and write poetry, fiction or an autobiography. There would be comfy old chairs and lots of tables that didn't need to be kept clean and we could even put some projects out on the big wraparound porch. Isn't it great, Tom?" Penny's flushed face and bright eyes were more than Tom could handle without showing some emotion and so he instinctively reached over to his wife of nineteen years, kissed her gently on both cheeks and held her close to his chest.

"Penny, I think it's a wonderful idea. What do you need me to help you do to make this dream a reality? I'll help in any way I can, baby. It's just wonderful to see you back to your old self, the way you were when we first got married and the kids were little." That night, Penny and Tom cooked dinner together and shared one of the good bottles of cabernet that they kept for special occasions as they talked through what needed to be done to purchase the old house, renovate it adequately and then start to fill it with all the arts and crafts materials that Penny had imagined. They made fresh spinach linguine with a tomato sauce made from the garden's last tomatoes and had a salad of fresh greens, broccoli, carrots and apples, tossed in olive oil and a balsamic vinegar from Italy that had been given to Penny as a hostess gift some time back. Tom and Penny had always loved cooking together and as they cooked, their ideas started to take shape and an action plan began to be formulated. As they sat down to dinner, Tom put his hand under Penny's chin and pulled her face up towards him. "I love you, sweetheart. Your happiness means the world to me." He kissed her softly on the lips and they sat down to dinner, holding hands and saying grace, thanking God for their many blessings and for the abundant joy that had filled their home, once again.

"I never really lost myself, even though it felt like it," thought Penny the next day as she drove to the local art supply store. "But if I felt lost, I know other women must be feeling the same way." She thought about women friends of hers, in all stages and phases of parenting and working, who were trying to juggle the demands of far too many different responsibilities and activities. "Find Yourself First. That's what I'll call my creativity center! That sends just the right message to all the women who put their own growth behind that of their kids and neglected their own learning until they finally became 'empty-nesters' and realized that their lives had lost enthusiasm, excitement and challenge. Just like mine did," she added honestly.

Penny arrived at the arts and crafts store and as she wandered the aisles, her mind began to run quickly through the various activities that could be part of the new women's creativity center, a place where she envisioned women would learn again how to express themselves fully. She imagined dance, music, yoga, creative writing, wood carving, pottery, quilting, knitting, painting and weaving workshops that could be taught by friends of hers who lived locally, as well as some who might be willing to fly in for a guest artist weekend workshop. This space would be a child-free zone but Penny imagined that there could be an adjacent building or someone's home where young children could be left with local teenage girls who wanted to babysit for extra money and they could set up some miniature painting easels and pottery play stations there as well. "What fun!" Penny thought blithely as her eye roamed across the colored pencils, pens, watercolors and art board in the aisle where she had stopped. She breathed a sigh of happiness and she contentedly began filling her cart.

Weeks later, over a cup of cappuccino at a neighborhood café, Penny tried to explain her feelings to her childhood best friend, Ellen. "It's amazing, Ellen," she said. "It feels as if I've been uplifted, inspired and renewed. I can't quite explain it, but the old feelings of tiredness, dread and emptiness that I used to feel on a daily basis have been replaced by a new sense of innocence and awe at the mystery of life."

Ellen looked closely at her friend Penny and noticed that she did indeed look more serene; perhaps innocent was the right word to describe her luminescent visage. Penny's tired eyes and dull skin had given way to two twinkling stars of light that, along with her translucent skin and shiny auburn hair, reflected the afternoon sunlight with an almost ephemeral quality. Ellen smiled, inviting Penny to continue. "It's as if my mind has been reawakened and all the creative possibilities I can imagine are swirling around inside my head constantly, just pulsing with light and life."

"Well, here's to life, then," said Ellen with an impish smile as she reached across the café table and gave Penny's hand a squeeze. "I'm so happy for you, Penny, and I know that your creativity center will bring joy to many, many more women in this little town. You were already a 'model Mommy'," she said with a little grin. "Now you'll be giving many more working mothers a true gift; you'll be giving them a deeper sense of self. I'm sure they're going to appreciate you so much, Penny." Penny blushed with humility as Ellen held out her hands again and found Penny's. Looking her square in the eyes, she said earnestly, "As for me, I appreciate you just because you're you and it's wonderful to have you back. Welcome back to yourself, Penny. Welcome home."

Chapter Ten

Physical Alchemy

Henny's Transformation

Henny sat at the typing table in her home office, early one Saturday morning, thinking about the book she was writing. This morning, she was specifically struggling with the incongruous truth that, paradoxically, developing her greatest strengths required that she admit to her greatest vulnerabilities, which in this case were almost entirely in the physical realm, and very much beyond her control. This internal conversation did not sit comfortably with her, but she pressed on with the writing because she knew that many, many other women needed to be able to have the very same internal conversation and she was providing them with a road map for how to begin it.

She paused from her philosophical musing to indulge her imagination about the impact her book would have on the millions of women she hoped would read it–women who desperately needed to take better care of their bodies. She smiled, acknowledging the current trend in books and articles targeting women's health; they focused almost exclusively on techniques to help them feel more sexually attractive and being physically fit was often viewed as a means to that end. "Nothing wrong with that," she thought, "but that's just not the whole story." Henny wanted her book to help women accept their vulnerabilities without feeling weak and defenseless, and to fully embrace their strengths, especially in the world of work, without being viewed by men as "ball busters" or Amazon women.

Henny had deftly walked the line between her feminine and masculine sides, especially at work, but she had never allowed vulnerability to be a part of either aspect of herself. Now, ironically, she wanted to guide others to realize what she had come to understand in her weakest and most vulnerable moments; namely, that her weakness was now the platform from which she would become her strongest self. She stared through her picture window into the early morning light that bathed her rose garden in its soft glow and thought about the trajectory her life had taken. She had grown from a hard-working child into a hard-working mother who almost simultaneously became a hard-working doctor. Now, she was becoming a vocal, nationally known advocate for rest, relaxation and self-care. "More than a bit incongruous," she again thought, ironically.

Henny realized that others might view her physical plight as one of deep misfortune or as an example of existential injustice, but she knew that her life had taken a new and powerful turn because of her diagnosis. Sure, she would have scripted a different life-changing event to get her to make that powerful turn; being stricken with MS was not what she would have chosen as the wake-up call to help her realize life didn't have to be such a struggle. "But we learn what we're taught," she thought consolingly. Life had certainly been an endless struggle for her parents and she had only had their relentless battling with circumstances as the template for what life was supposed to be like. She felt deeply sad that they had experienced such poverty, discrimination and strife in their lives, but she knew plenty of upper-middle-class women who also struggled endlessly—compulsively driving themselves to the brink of exhaustion, trying to keep up with somebody or something, every day, all of their lives—so she knew that struggle was a fundamental part of the human condition, no matter what the circumstances were.

As a case in point, her own beloved daughter, Tessie, had slid for a mercifully brief, but very terrifying, period of time into a severe eating disorder as she tried to be the perfectly shaped, straight-A college student. Fortunately, Henny had recognized the telltale signs and had gotten Tessie into some much-needed therapy before she spiraled too far down into the pit of restrictive eating. Henny lamented the cold hard truth that the social pressures on girls and young women to be perfect were intense. Then there were the over-achieving middle-aged women, like her, who were trying way too hard to be pillars of strength for everybody else, often neglecting themselves in the process. "Why did it take a two-by-four between the eyes to wake me up to this pattern of incessant striving?" she thought, sadly.

Henny was deep in thought about the cultural pressures on women and the message she wanted to deliver to them via her book when she heard a knock at the door. Henny knew that Carlos had already gone off to the hospital to prep for an early surgery. The housekeeper, Tanya, had been to the house the day before so she knew it couldn't be her. It was too early for any of her friends to be dropping by for coffee and her kids, Tessie and Henry were both in NYC, or so she thought. As she sat thinking about who could be knocking, the door slowly opened and she saw Tessie poking her head around the corner. "Baby!" exclaimed, Henny, "What on earth are you doing home?"

It was the middle of Tessie's second semester in med school at NYU and there was no way she could have found a way to steal home for a weekend, given the amount of work Henny knew first year med students had to complete. Tessie walked into her mother's office and as Henny stood up to move towards her, she could see the bags under her uncharacteristically mascara-free eyes, her hair in an unkempt ponytail and her still thin body clad in baggy sweatpants. She looked like an orphan or a waif, certainly not like a first year medical student. "Oh, Mom!" Tessie wailed as she rushed into her mother's arms and buried her head in Henny's bosom. She just stood there, sobbing, while Henny stroked her hair and murmured soothing words to calm her. After about five minutes of heavy crying, Tessie started to catch her breath with gulps of air and a few yawns and then became quiet and looked pathetically up at her mother's face with the look of a small child needing consoling.

Henny knew better than to start asking questions yet. She firmly took Tessie by the hand and walked with her into the kitchen where she put on a kettle of water for tea and started to warm up some cinnamon buns she had made for breakfast the day before. She bustled about, taking charge and letting Tessie feel cared for while the easy quiet spaces between them settled gently like a soft morning fog. Henny had a brief flashback to a time, many years ago, when she used to make dinner in the kitchen while Tessie would sit silently at the kitchen island and simply watch. This ritual always soothed Tessie when she became too stressed with her studies or boyfriend problems and this was exactly what she needed now. Henny poured the hot water over some loose Earl Gray tea leaves in Tessie's favorite tea pot, got some half and half out, pulled the buns from the oven and placed one on a small plate for Tessie, along with a napkin and a fork.

Tessie gratefully poured herself some tea after it had steeped for a several minutes, added a touch of cream and took a slow sip, with her eyes closed. "Time enough to hear the story," thought Henny patiently, although she couldn't keep her intuitive mothering instincts from rifling through all the possible disasters that Tessie could have encountered. After about fifteen minutes, the color began to come back to Tessie's tear-stained face and she attempted a slight smile as her mother sat down next to her on a kitchen stool and looked at her expectantly. "Okay, honey, let's hear the story," said Henny, prompting Tessie to begin what had all the signs of a very painful narrative.

Tessie breathed a sigh as she sipped her tea and started to speak. "Mom, I'm so embarrassed. I could just die. I can't believe what has happened to me. I used to have everything so together." Henny knew better than to probe or interject any questions so she just sat silently, waiting. "I've not been honest with you about how things have been going at med school, Mom. It's actually been really awful. Last semester I struggled to keep up with the coursework and finished all but one of my classes, which I took an incomplete in. The professor said I could complete the research paper over Christmas break, but I was so exhausted when I came home, that I just couldn't make myself do it." Tessie paused to see if there was any judgment in Henny's eyes but she only saw the warm look of compassion that she knew so well.

"So, when I returned for the second semester, I talked to the professor and she said I could have one more month to get the paper done. I kept meaning to get it done, but then the coursework in second semester just seemed to pile on and I couldn't keep up with any of it. I started to stay up way too late to try and get the work done and then I got so tired that I fell asleep in class a few times. One of my classmates noticed and suggested that I go speak with the Dean, but I just couldn't do that. I would have died of shame."

Henny continued to listen, not saying a word. "So, then, Mom, I started to take NoDoz pills to keep myself up and I started to restrict my food again and I just ground myself down into a complete wreck. Finally, I knew I couldn't keep up with any of the classes and I did go to the Dean and asked what he could do to help me. He said that the only option at this stage in the game was to give me a medical leave of absence and I could take the rest of the term off, finish up the paper for last semester so I don't lose the credit and then start all over again in the fall, with the new incoming first year class." Tessie stopped and looked at her mother, anxiously, for signs of a response.

"Are you disappointed in me, Mom?" said Tessie, tear-fully, as she drew her story to a close. "I'm so sorry. I know how proud you and Dad were when I got into med school and how happy you were that I wanted to be a doctor like you two. I just don't know if I've got what it takes, Mom. I'm scared that I'm not tough enough to do this." At this admission of her feelings of failure and weakness, Tessie began to cry again and Henny stood up and moved over to Tessie's stool and cradled her daughter's head in her arms. They stood like that for a while and then Henny took Tessie's hand and drew her into the living room where she sank into the big comfy sofa and pulled Tessie down next to her.

Henny took her time as she composed a response in her mind. This was an opportunity for her to share her message of rest and renewal with Tessie. She didn't want to sound patronizing, however, nor did she want Tessie to feel as if she had given up on her. Henny took a deep breath and started speaking in her kind, warm voice. "Tessie baby, I'm not disappointed in you at all. You're my darling child and my delight and you have never disappointed me. I'm very sad that you've had such a hard time over the past several months and that you didn't feel like you could ask your Dad or me to help you out. That does make me sad, but I totally understand that you wanted to try to figure out a solution on your own, without us rescuing you. I admire your courage, honey, but I have to tell you I'm worried by your inability to slow down and take care of yourself."

Henny paused here as she thought about how to phrase her next thoughts. "Tessie, I owe you an apology. I've taught you how to wear yourself out, push yourself to the point of exhaustion and ignore what your body is telling you. I've taught you that you could be a young superwoman, a perfect daughter, a perfect student, a perfect model-thin beauty. I am so very sorry, sweetheart. I am so very, very sorry." Tessie looked at her mother through the tears in her lashes with an expression of surprise and confusion. "You're sorry, Mom? Why? I don't get it. I'm the one who let you down. I'm the one who couldn't hack it. I'm the failure."

Henny put her finger to Tessie's lips to shush her. "No, baby, you're not the one who let me down. I've been teaching you since you were old enough to know what your name was that you could be great, that you could do anything you set your mind to, that you could handle anything life threw in your path. What I didn't teach you was how to slow down, rest and care for your poor little body and your tired mind and spirit. I didn't teach you that because I didn't know how to do that myself. In fact, it's taken a major medical crisis to get me to reassess how I think about success and happiness and what living the good life really means."

"I've led you off a high cliff, honey, and I need to help you figure out how to open your parachute and land on a sandy beach. Your father and I will help you figure out how to handle school, if you want to go back, but for now, I want to just hold my baby girl in my arms and let you know that I'm very proud of you, I love you, I think you're amazing and wonderful and talented, and you have done nothing to make me feel anything less than total joy at being able to be your mother. Thank you, my sweet Tessie. Thank you." Henny was the one crying at this point, as she drew her apology to a close.

Tessie sat in quiet, stunned amazement and finally pulled her thoughts together enough to speak. "Mom, are you telling me that you're apologizing for my failure? Are you telling me that it's all okay and you're not mad at me?" Henny nodded in assent. "Wow, Mom. I don't know what to say, except thank you. I thought you were going to be so sad and disappointed in me. Do you think Dad will be upset?" Henny gave her daughter a squeeze and said, "In the past few months, your daddy has learned a few of the same lessons, sweetheart. Don't worry about him. He'll be fine and he loves you as much as I do. Now, I want you to go get a shower, put on something that makes you feel pretty and you and I are going to go out for a long walk to have some time just to share what's really been going on inside that beautiful mind of yours. I want to know everything, Tessie, every little thing."

As Tessie gave her mother another grateful hug and got up to go take a shower, Henny pondered the amazing serendipity of her daughter's breakdown at just this point, when Henny needed to put something personal in her book about self-care and self-love. She paused and then a smile lit up her face. She had a crazy thought, but it might just work. In about thirty minutes, Tessie re-emerged, her blown-dry mahogany hair falling softly against her face and her cute figure clothed in some trendy jeans, t-shirt and a stylish jacket. She clearly had gotten a little spring back in her step, and for this, Henny was deeply grateful.

"Tessie," said Henny, "I have an idea I'd like to run by you. You know I've been working on a book about women and self-care based on my experience with MS, don't you?" Tessie nodded. "Well, baby, now that you have the rest of the spring term to hang out, what would you think about helping me with the book by writing a chapter about your own experience at med school?" Tessie looked at Henny with horrified eyes. "Share about my crash and burn scenario, Mom? That's not exactly very flattering." Henny smiled quietly and said, "Honey, you're wrong. You're an incredibly strong, gifted, courageous young woman. You should be proud of who you are. And if you're honest, you can tell your story so that other young women like you can learn from your experience and you can start to teach about self-care and renewal alongside me, but you can speak to your own generation of women in your own way. I'd love to have you come to some of my conferences and share your story. Would you like to do that with me?"

Henny waited quietly while all kinds of emotions played across Tessie's face. Finally, Tessie looked her mom straight in the eyes, and said in a strong, firm voice, "Yes, Mom. I would. I definitely would." With that, the two women linked arms and headed for the door to take a long walk in the early morning air, feeling the freshness of spring and new life on their faces and smelling the rich, pungent odor of damp earth. "Now I know what 'hope springs eternal' means, Mom," said Tessie as she gave her mother a beautiful smile and started to skip and then to whistle and then to laugh, gently at first and then harder until the tears were flowing from her eyes and smearing all of her new makeup. "I love you, Mom. I just love you," said Tessie with exuberance and childlike adoration. "I love you too, Tessie, my sweet. I love you too."

Epilogue: Receiving

"All you have to do is float."
– Martha Beck

It's another January, fourteen years later. Balmy breezes blow through my hair and kiss my face as I walk down the street to get a cappuccino and ponder my own story of emotional alchemy. I survey the current stats on my life and feel a deep sense of gratitude for all the blessings that have accrued over the past fourteen years since my visit with my mother in the hospital.

The years have been fraught with struggle and replete with "growth opportunities" that I have resolutely trudged my way through, often questioning why I always seem to have to learn things the hard way. But now, things don't seem so hard to me. When I look at my life from a distance, I see a gentle meadow with grasses blowing in the wind, a gorgeous tree standing watch over me as I lean against its rugged bark and feel the peace of knowing there is nowhere else I'd rather be. I see a lack of drama. I see time spent with the ones I love and an early avoidance of the ones I don't. I speak my truth as often as I can, mustering whatever courage is necessary to say what needs to be said. I pursue moments of simplicity. I avoid struggle. I work on floating and not pushing the river. Joy, peace, beauty and truth have become my mantra.

My alchemy is my work and my work is having conversations with people who are at all different stages of learning how to find their own alchemical processes. I love my work with every fiber of my soul. I work in a big, beautiful, hundred-year-old home, a remnant of Durham's tobacco-rich culture with fireplaces, wide, heart pine floors and a soul. I've decorated it with dark, rich colors and comfortable sofas and chairs for settling in and talking at length, the way we did before the internet, before the television, before the cell phone, before email. I help my clients remember who they are through conversation and while I'm at it, I love them, accept them and lead them towards the right questions for their own lives, not mine.

I love having the opportunity to sit with people in the midst of their confusion, trials and tribulations and to empathize, sympathize and exercise my gift for using metaphor to teach them about who they are. I love working with words, both spoken and written. Words are the colors that I paint with to help each person create their own complex and beautiful canvas. Choices are the tools that I help them make with skill. Personal responsibility becomes the rule of thumb: if you don't like where you are, then have the courage to change where you are. Hoping someone will fix it for you or give you permission to fix it isn't part of the game. Consequences are the teachers that go hand in hand with choices and they are sometimes hard to swallow. But each consequence fully experienced leads to the possibility of a new alchemy, a new regenerative moment. In each of those moments of consequence, my starfish draw upon their own power of regeneration to grow new rays from the broken ones and thus, a new starfish leader is born.

Starfish leaders have experienced the shattering realization that their most cherished values have collapsed under them. They learn that they must regenerate themselves through a long and painful process of reflection about who they are, who they are not, and who they want to be. After answering these questions as only they can, they move into the alchemical phase of leading where they turn the dross of their lives into gold by accepting what is so, rather than what they wish were so and by permitting their weathered spirits to receive the gifts of wisdom that come to them, often through times of great pain. Starfish leaders grow by continuously accepting the unfolding truth of their lives. They learn how to rejoice in the simple beauty of a day well lived and of people well loved. Starfish leaders are strong in the broken places and at peace in the midst of their human frailties.

I wish for all of you readers the courage to claim your lives and make them fully your own. I challenge you to find your own truth, to ask your own questions, to be your own person. I hope that by candidly sharing some of my experience, I have let you know that I am not perfect and I have not figured everything out. I have simply dedicated myself to the process of uncovering what brings joy, peace, beauty and truth into my life. I wish for you the chance to dedicate yourself to your own process of uncovering and fulfilling who you were meant to be. I wish you joy, peace, beauty and truth as you turn your life into gold, as you embrace the brokenness that befalls each one of us, and as you permit your spirit to become whole again.

The Starfish Leader©

A Questionnaire

Starfish Leaders are those who continually invest their time in the process of self-discovery and self-awareness. You may be a leader in your family, school, community, family-owned business, entrepreneurial start-up, church, university, hospital, non-profit charitable organization or in a large multi-national corporation. It matters not. Imagine that you are a Starfish Leader and just like a starfish, your entire life is divided naturally and equally into five rays: spiritual, material, emotional, intellectual and physical. Now imagine that your ability to lead is only as effective as your ability to keep your starfish rays whole. Most of us who have walked along the edge of the ocean have seen starfish with broken tips and sometimes, even entire rays missing, but usually they are whole. Have you ever wondered why?

One of the wonders of starfish is that they can regenerate their broken arms and make themselves whole again. There are not many organisms on this earth that have the power to do that. While we humans cannot regenerate missing or destroyed limbs, we are able to regenerate these five "arms" in our lives, but sometimes we're not sure what needs to be regenerated or we're not even aware that anything is broken until life comes crashing down around us. This set of questions is designed to help you become aware of those elements of your life where you are whole and healthy and those areas where you are chipped or broken and in need of healing. Do you know where you need help in regenerating yourself so that your leadership can flourish?

Start by answering the following questions. These will help you identify where you might want to step back, take stock and regenerate broken or incomplete parts of your life so that your leadership can emerge from a place of grounded completeness. Then continue the conversation with someone you trust and whose wisdom you can learn from, so that you can continue to grow into a more complete and beautiful star.

Directions:
1. Answer each question with a yes or a no in your journal and then honestly dive into the explanation for your answers.

2. Give clear examples from your life to illustrate all the yes answers in detail.

3. Celebrate these answers with someone you love.

4. Create action steps to move you to yes on the no answers.

5. You may wish to use some of the following "re" words to help you create your action steps: reassemble, replenish, refine, redefine, renegotiate, rethink, renew, rebuild, readjust, rebalance, recover, realign, reconsider, reignite, reeducate, release, remove, remember, redo, reintegrate, reenergize, redouble, reflect, remind.

6. Share these steps with someone who can help you be accountable to yourself.

7. Revisit this test whenever you feel that your life is out of balance or not working well, to see where you may need to harness the power of regeneration.

The Five Rays of the Starfish Leader

<u>Your Intellectual-Professional Ray</u>   <u>Yes</u>   <u>No</u>

Are you challenged intellectually and professionally?

Do you think new thoughts on a frequent basis?

Do you feel stimulated in your chosen career or life path?

Are you being consistently creative?

Are you making the world a better place in which to live?

Are you using your intellectual gifts and talents optimally?

Actions to take:

1.

2.

3.

Your Physical-Sensual Ray   Yes   No

Do you nurture your body on a daily basis?

Do you rest your body adequately every night?

Do you feel comfortable in your skin?

Do you move your body often, actively and with pleasure?

Do you indulge your body's five senses on a regular basis?

Do you get physical touch frequently in a safe environment?

Actions to take:

1.

2.

3.

Your Emotional-Relational Ray   <u>Yes</u>   <u>No</u>

Do you feel emotionally alive?

Do you have intimate conversations on a regular basis?

Do you trust others enough to be open with them?

Do you share your feelings freely with others?

Do you express love easily and often?

Do you have deeply fulfilling relationships with others?

Actions to take:

1.

2.

3.

Your Spiritual-Metaphysical Ray   <u>Yes</u>   <u>No</u>

Do you often feel deeply peaceful?

Do you appreciate each moment as a miraculous gift?

Are you filled with gratitude and awe for the gift of life?

Do you fully appreciate and marvel at nature?

Do you feel complete, whole, fulfilled and content?

Do you believe in and feel loved by God?

Actions to take:

1.

2.

3.

<u>Your Material-Financial Ray</u>   <u>Yes</u>   <u>No</u>

Do you feel wealthy?

Do you have every "thing" you really want in life?

Are you financially secure and unconcerned about a money crisis?

Do you understand what money can do and can't do?

Are you willing to share your money with others less fortunate?

Do you use money to bring more joy into your own and others' lives?

Actions to take:

1.

2.

3.

Regenerating Your Rays

Here are some ideas to help you regenerate your rays. Use these to spur your thinking about possible things you can do to make your life more whole.

Answer the following sentence stems with possible actions you can take.

Starting today, I will:

Replenish my spirit by

_____

Refine my thinking by

_____

Relive good memories by

_____

Redefine what matters most by

_____

Renegotiate a commitment by

_____

Rethink a plan by

_____

Renew a promise by

_____

Rebuild a dream by

_____

Readjust my expectations by

_____

Rebalance my life by

_____

Recover my sense of humor by

_____

Realign my priorities by

_____

Reconsider an opportunity by

_____

Reignite a passion by

_____

Reeducate my mind by

_____

Release my grievances by

_____

Remove my filters by

_____

Remember my intentions by

_____

Redo a failed attempt by

_____

Reintegrate my work and relationships by

_____

Reenergize my exercise by

_____

Redouble my efforts by

_____

Reflect my best qualities by

_____

Readdress unfinished business by

_____

Remind myself I am loved by

_____

Redress a wrong by

_____

Relieve my chronic tension by

_____

Recreate my childhood by

_____

If you wish to contact the author about speaking opportunities, executive coaching, seminars or retreats you may use any of the following:

   address: 514 South Duke Street ~ Durham, NC 27701
   email: rebecca@merrillleadership.com
   phone: 919-619-1369
   author website: www.rebeccamerrill.com
   executive coaching website: www.merrillleadership.com

Additional copies of Starfish Leaders may be ordered through www.amazon.com, www.borders.com, www.barnesandnoble .com or your local independent book store.

LaVergne, TN USA
01 September 2010
195445LV00002B/8/P